Mary Ann Bishop has sounded a clarion call for all individuals who call themselves Christian and all churches proclaiming the name of Jesus Christ. We are called to realize and re-discover our true purpose, identity, and joyful blessing as missionaries and mission centers, reaching all nations with the gospel of Jesus Christ, the Savior of the world. May we joyfully accept God's call to Jonah—and to us—to reach everyone, everywhere, with the good news of Jesus' love, grace, and forgiveness!

> DR. WAYNE AND JOY BROWN
> Co-Founders of Diversified Ministries

It has been said that the question is not how many good books have you read, but rather, how many good books have you mastered. *Jonah, God's Reluctant Prophet* is a book that should be mastered by both those in pulpits and those in the pews, for never has the story of Jonah been more relevant to the contemporary church than at this juncture in human history. Mary Ann Bishop masterfully brings the story of Jonah alive and reminds us of the purpose of our election: to lovingly bring the message of the gospel to a world that otherwise is without hope. This is a read that will deepen your theology, enrich your biblical history, challenge you to search your own motives and inspire your devotion to make Christ known to the Nations. This will be a perennial read in my library.

> DR. TED SHERRILL
> Senior Pastor, First Baptist Church, Georgetown, SC

Jonah, God's Reluctant Prophet, by Mary Ann Bishop is filled with thorough historical and cultural background, without losing sight of how God works deeply in Jonah's heart and has a penetrating word to Israel and to all believers today. Mary Ann shows us how God's assignment to Jonah and God's response to Jonah's racially prideful rebellion is a teachable moment for all of His people. She wisely focuses on the penetrating questions God poses to Jonah to expose the motives and beliefs of all of God's followers. Use this study to guide others into actively engaging God's mission.

> DR. ROY KING
> Professor Emeritus, Columbia International University Seminary
> Leadership Coach/ Organizational Consultant

When Jesus was on earth, he spoke of only a few prophets by name, one of them was Jonah, who was a sign of Jesus' death and resurrection. Jonah's life and words are timely for all ages. Mary Ann Bishop has masterfully brought the book of Jonah to life, and constructed a life-applicational study that needs to be read and studied by twenty-first century Christians.

DR. PHILIP COMFORT
Senior Bible Reference Editor and Author, Tyndale House Publishers
New Testament Editor for the New Living Translation
Professor of Greek and New Testament

Mary Ann Bishop's book, *Jonah, God's Reluctant Prophet,* is an accurate EKG of God's heart beat for missions. As a cross-cultural missionary for 33 years, I personally know Mary Ann Bishop's sacrificial commitment and unique contribution to missions. I greatly admire her passionate love for our great nation India. Year after year, she travels across continents with her teams to train leaders in missions and churches. She is in sync with the God of Jonah. For her, Jonah is not merely an ancient narrative or an abstract message but real life and experience. I greatly respect when lifestyle matches words. Here we meet an author who in personal lifestyle "runs with God" and has penned words for our missionary God. I am greatly honored and excited to recommend this book.

REV. A. MALAR SELVAN, M. DIV.
Founder and Director, Apostolic Good News Ministries, Jabalpur, India

The books written by Mary Ann Bishop under the major title *Servants of the Most High God* not only create passion for reaching those who remain unreached, but offer courage to stand up to the rising opposition against the gospel so prevalent in South Asia. These materials are helpful in teaching believers in three significant areas of Christian discipleship and leadership: first, through the teaching of sound biblical doctrines, second, through the teaching of godly character, and third, through the teaching of a Christ centered lifestyle and witness. Every story is biblically authentic and practically effective in training and developing disciples and leaders for church planting movements around the world. We have utilized these materials to train pastors, evangelists, women leaders, church elders and children alike. I highly recommend *Jonah, God's Reluctant Prophet* as a resource that will deepen your faith and equip you for God's service.

REV. DR. S. D. PONRAJ
South Asia Coordinator, Servants Network of South Asia
Author and Publisher, Mission Educational Books, India
Former Senior Pastor, Bihar Christian Church, Bihar, India

JONAH

GOD'S RELUCTANT PROPHET

JONAH

GOD'S RELUCTANT PROPHET

Mary Ann Bishop

Tallgrass Media

Columbia, South Carolina

Jonah: God's Reluctant Prophet
Copyright © 2020 by Mary Ann Bishop

Published by Tallgrass Media
Columbia, South Carolina
books@tallgrass.media
www.tallgrassmedia.com

Cover and interior book design by Kelly Smith.
Cover artwork by April Bensch.

Printed in the United States of America
First printing, 2020.

ISBN-13: 978-0-9997626-5-3

To my friend and mission partner, S.D. Ponraj

How is it possible to measure all you have taught me through both word and example over the course of more than a decade? I have watched your life closely, walked beside you, and worked with you for the glory of God. You have opened countless doors of opportunity allowing me to fulfill the desire of my heart to reach the nations for Christ. I offer you my heartfelt thanks for showing me the heart of a genuine missionary for which I am eternally grateful.

Contents

xiii   Preface

xxi   Introduction

STORY 1   RUNNING FROM GOD — JONAH 1

3   Chapter 1 — God Calls Jonah to Ninevah

17   Chapter 2 — The Depravity of Ninevah and a Prophet's Heart

29   Chapter 3 — The Storm of a Lifetime

44   Recap

STORY 2   RUNNING TO GOD — JONAH 2

49   Chapter 4 — Jonah's Despair and Desperation

67   Chapter 5 — Jonah's Dedication and Deliverance

85   Chapter 6 — Greater Miracles and Lesser Miracles

96   Recap

STORY 3   RUNNING WITH GOD — JONAH 3

101   Chapter 7 — Jonah's Re-Commission

113   Chapter 8 — God's Command to Ninevah

127   Chapter 9 — Jonah's Effect Upon Ninevah

138   Recap

STORY 4   RUNNING INTO GOD — JONAH 4

143   Chapter 10 — God Relents, Ninevah Repents, and Jonah Resents

159   Chapter 11 — Jonah's Anger Prompts God's Questions

175   Chapter 12 — God Expresses His Compassion for All People

183   Recap

187   Conclusion

202   Bibliography

205   About the Author

Three Reasons You Need Jesus

Jesus loves you! He desires to have a relationship with you, and to give you a life full of joy and purpose. Why do you need Him in your life?

1.   Because You Have a Past

You can't go back, but He can. The Bible says, "Jesus Christ is the same yesterday, and today, and forever" (Hebrews 13:8). He can walk into those places of sin and failure, wipe the slate clean, and give you a brand new beginning.

2.   Because You Need a Friend

Jesus knows the worst about you, yet He believes the best. Why? Because He sees you not as you are but as you will be when He gets through with You. What a friend we have in Jesus!

3.   Because He Holds the Future

Who else are you going to trust? In His hands you are safe and secure—today, tomorrow, and for all eternity. His Word says, "For I know the plans I have for you . . . plans for good and not for evil, to give you a future and a hope. In those days when you pray, I will listen" (Jeremiah 29:11–12).

If you would like to begin a personal relationship with Jesus today, please pray this prayer:

Lord Jesus, I invite You into my life.
I believe You died for me and that Your blood pays
For my sins and provides me with the gift of eternal life.
By faith I receive that gift,
and I acknowledge You are my Lord and Savior. Amen.
(Taken from: *The Word For You Today*. Celebration, Inc., 2018)

Preface

Our Missionary God

The God of the Old Testament not only identifies Himself as the God of Abraham, Isaac and Jacob, but also disclosed to Moses His personal name, Yahweh, and from the beginning declares Himself the God of the whole world. As early as Genesis 10, we are presented with a list of all the nations of the earth confirming the truth that they arise from the creative hand of Almighty God, and stand under His watchful eye of both mercy and judgment. From the earliest biblical records, it is evident that God's work and activity are directed at the whole of humanity. This is one of the fundamental truths of the account presented in Genesis 1–11 and the record of history's beginning. It is likewise found in the account of history's ending recorded in the book of Revelation. The same God who revealed Himself to Old Testament Israel dwelt among us in Jesus Christ in the days of the Roman Empire and identifies Himself as the Alpha and Omega, The Beginning and The End. The Bible clearly declares that He does not lay down His work until "every tongue and nation" and a "multitude without number" have been gathered round His throne. God is clearly cutting a path through the confusing activities of mankind throughout all history in order to achieve His redemptive goals among the nations—among all peoples.

God's People and God's Son

At first glance, this God of the whole world appears to narrow His interests to the private history of one family, but nothing could be further from the truth. For a time, the nation of Israel, descendants of the family of Abraham, were separated from other nations, but only so that God could pave the way in achieving His world-embracing goals. God never took His eye off other nations although Israel was the "apple of His eye," a minority nation, called to serve the majority. God's election of Israel, therefore, concerned the whole world. In order to speak to the world in the fullness of time, God needed a people—His servants, His ambassadors, His nation—upholding His truth and representing His character. Therefore, God chose Israel as the key player in His eventual completion of His universal intentions.

God's intention is always to save and to deliver. His glory is on display in all He does, and He acts so that His great name might be exalted among the nations. Isaiah 53 unveils the secret of precisely *how* the Servant of the Lord (Jesus Christ) would discharge His mission of bringing God's deliverance and salvation to the world. Written 600 years before the actual event, this passage graphically depicts God's Servant (Christ) becoming a victim of the most savage human butchery. Every kind of mistreatment the human mind could possibly devise would be done to Him. However, the Servant is prophesied in Isaiah 53 as a substitute who willingly incurs the wrath and judgment of God which was properly due not only to Israel but to all peoples and nations. Most significant is the fact that Isaiah beautifully describes *the nations* as the Father's gifts to His Son, the Servant, in return for His sacrificial obedience to suffer death on mankind's behalf. Jesus Christ, therefore, achieved the right as God's suffering Servant to bring salvation and healing to all people of all nations.

Israel's Mission: To Represent God

The prophets of the Old Testament never tired of reminding Israel that her election was not a privilege which she could selfishly keep for herself, but rather a calling to service that carried great responsibility. Israel's calling involved a God-given duty to be a light among the nations—a living representative of the truth of the Most High God. Israel was to live as the people of God among the godless nations in order to show them God's unique grace, mercy and salvation. Time and time again the prophets recorded their deep disappointment in Israel's willful disobedience and ongoing rebellion. God's mandate was that Israel be a transforming presence among the nations living as a distinct people and a royal priesthood, for a godly life is one of the most effective methods of engaging the culture and the world. Through the very act of living out her divine assignment as a people set apart to God, Israel was to be a sign of the reality of this living God—a bridge for the nations to experience the saving love of the Most High God.

There were a striking number of individuals whose biblical stories reveal the abandonment of their heathen origins, and by the simplicity of word and deed through the witnesses of the Most High God, they were won over to trust and serve the one true and living God. The stories of Melchizedek, Abraham, Rahab, Ruth, Job, and the people of Nineveh described in the book of Jonah, along with many others are windows through which we may look out onto the vast expanse of people outside the nation of Israel. Through their powerful stories of transformation, we can hear the faint strains of the missionary call sounding forth to all people. The concluding chapter of Jonah resonates with this very truth:

The glory of Yahweh-Adonai shall be revealed among *all peoples*. Then every human being shall come to know Him as He really is, the "gracious and merciful God, slow to anger and abounding in steadfast love, and relenting from disaster" (Jonah 4:2).

Jonah's Reluctance: God's Mercy

The book of Jonah is unlike all other prophetic writings in the sense that the prophets of God ordinarily relayed little about their personal lives and instead, focused on God's message of repentance and impending judgment. Because Jonah's first response to God's call was rebellion, the record of his ministry became an intensely personal story of his struggle to obey God and come to terms with his acceptance of God's incomprehensible mercy toward a pagan, cruel and godless nation. The story of Jonah is a sobering lesson in what it means to be a missionary. There must be a radical conversion of one's natural tendencies and a complete restructuring of one's life in order to achieve proper alignment with the greater purposes of God. In Jonah, the will of one man and the will of the one true God collide, with the man being brought to the point of a critical decision: "Will I accept that God is God and yield my will to His, or will I continue to resist the truth of His deep mercy toward all peoples?"

The Bible is not afraid of reporting real life experiences as messy, ugly and confusing, as they often are. In the story of Jonah, God's specially-chosen prophet is portrayed with no sugarcoating. His willful disobedience and defiance toward God is on grand display. The book does not end "happily ever after" as we might wish, but concludes with God's probing into the prideful heart of His servant, who wrestles to the bitter end over God's purposes to deliver, save and include all people in His unfolding redemptive plan. God's final question to Jonah lingers in the air as we too contemplate our own prideful and presumptuous hearts:

". . . And should I not pity Nineveh . . . ?" (4:11)

Probing Questions for All Times

What can a book like Jonah possibly mean for the twenty-first century world of our day today—a world of convenience, comfort, pleasure and ever-changing technology? The issues addressed in this book are incredibly relevant for the present generation. Our God never changes, and His truth is timeless. He is the same yesterday, today and forever, and His purposes and plans for this world remain intact and on course just as they did in Jonah's day.

The writer unapologetically sets forth Jonah's futile attempt to undermine God's worldwide redemptive plans so that readers today can hear and apply the same lessons. Most scholars concur that Jonah himself wrote the narrative in autobiographical fashion but simply used the common biblical practice of writing in third person. In any case, the author may have left the book open-ended—with no record of the prophet's answer to His question or any evidence of final repentance for a very specific purpose. The 48 verses of this small book contain no less than 14 questions, 11 of which are directed at Jonah, and by extension to you and me—the reader today.

Jonah's continuing struggle examines multiple issues and probes deeply the mysterious character of the Most High God. The book portrays human rebellion and God's response to it in vivid color. Along the way, the reader learns through Jonah's negative example that knowing God and choosing to follow His will are vitally important matters—if one is ever to be useful in advancing the global purposes of God. The people of Nineveh were sinners desperately lost apart from God's grace. Yet ironically, so was Jonah . . . and so are we. God's greatest desire was to restore Jonah to a place of sweet fellowship and maximum usefulness. Perhaps most significant, however, is the refreshing insight into the character of our loving and merciful God. He is long-suffering and full of compassion. There are no lost causes with Him. No one is beyond His reach or His love. Likewise, He longs for His people to extend to this lost world the same loving-kindness each has received from Him.

Are You Jonah?

Jonah is a story not soon to be forgotten. It challenges the reader to "test and evaluate yourselves to see whether you are in the faith and living your lives as believers" (2 Corinthians 13:5). It portrays the sin of a prideful ambassador of the Most High God whose heart is simply not in the assignment. Angry that God shows mercy to the nations, the deep-seated issues of the prophet's heart come rolling out of his mouth as he arrogantly vents his fury in the form of a final prayer found in the last chapter of the book. These telling words comprise the key text of the entire book, highlighting the beauty of God's mercy while striking like a venomous serpent at the selfishness and arrogance so commonly found in the human heart:

"And he (Jonah) prayed to the Lord and said, 'O Lord, is not this what I said when I was yet in my country? That is why I made haste to flee to Tarshish; for I knew that you are a gracious God and merciful, slow to anger and abounding in steadfast love, and relenting from disaster.'" (Jonah 4:2)

Jonah's prayer reveals that he simply could not stand to think that God treats those outside the covenant in the same way He treats those within it. What resides in the heart comes out of the mouth. His words reveal his obstinate refusal to acknowledge the covenant's universal purpose—to bring salvation to the worldwhich certainly includes the heathen. The truth of the matter is simply this: both Israel and the Gentiles alike live by the unmerited grace that the Creator gives to all of his creatures. Therefore, God responded to His prophet no longer as a covenant partner—but as the Creator of all and asks His pouting creature: "What right do you have, Jonah, to be angry?"

The Compelling Beauty of Our Great God

By the end of the book it is obvious that God's patience with his stiff-necked missionary is exhausted. What did God see in this man, and why is his story so needful to twenty-first century believers today? He obviously failed every test. He did not see the point of the violent storm, nor the commendable actions of the sailors. He failed to recognize the providential appearance of the great fish that arrived at the perfect time in the perfect place to preserve his life. Nor did he see the point of Nineveh's remarkable conversion in spite of his reluctantly delivered message. He did not see the point of these things simply because he did not want to see them. The final question to Jonah leaves the reader to ponder the ugliness of prideful arrogance so common to the human experience.

From the study of Jonah's life, we learn that God spares and God rescues. We also see that He judges and He relents. He is God and He does as He will. Israel's God is Nineveh's God as well. There is only one true and living God—the Most High God, and unlike Jonah, the Most High God has no "Gentile prejudice." While He never forces Himself upon any one, He tenderly pursues and draws us to Himself compelling us to put our whole heart and soul into His purposes and the work of His mission, even when we do not understand it. God is still committed to the transformation of obstinate, irritable, negative thinking, biased Jonahs and turning them into powerful, Spirit-filled ambassadors of the Gospel which alone brings freedom to those still enslaved in the clutches of sin.

In the end, God accomplished His purpose for the city of Nineveh for He always achieves His purposes. Indeed, there was a witness to the Ninevites of His truth. But for Jonah, an unsettling question remains. The book has no conclusion and the final question asked receives no answer, except from those who have read this same question down through the ages and who accept without questioning the justice of a merciful God and His inexhaustible grace. Our gracious God is searching for servants who will actively answer the same missionary call to share the free gift of His salvation with a lost and ever-darkening world. Will He find such a servant in you? In me? The question begs for an answer. The book of Jonah is the missionary call to every believer to finish the task! Will you accept the commission? Will you go?

The Sobering Challenge For Us All

The Church of the twenty-first century must pay close attention to this sobering message for Jesus Christ claimed to be the "One greater than Jonah" (Matthew 12:39–41; Luke 11:29–32). His death on the cross with its awful cry of God forsaking Him, His three days in the tomb as Jonah was three days in the fish, and His glorious resurrection with its jubilant shout of victory are all signs of Jonah for us today, each pointing to the profound meaning of His whole life and clearly attesting that God indeed loves the whole world so much that He gave His only Son, Jesus, to prove it. Therefore, if one draws his lifeblood from the One greater than Jonah and yet refuses to spread among the lost the good news of salvation of this one and only Savior—he too, like Jonah, is sabotaging the purposes of God Himself. Jonah, therefore, is the father to all who desire the benefits and blessing of their election but who refuse its responsibility. May the reader study and meditate upon these stories allowing God's probing questions to examine and expose the remaining pride, prejudice, disobedience and rebellion still stubbornly embedded in the hearts of each of us.

"You Jonah"

And Jonah stalked
to his shaded seat
and waited for God
to come around
to his way of thinking.
And God is still waiting
for a host of Jonahs
in their comfortable houses
to come around
to His way of loving.

Thomas Carlisle

NOTES

Thoughts in this preface taken from: Verkuyl, Johannes. "The Biblical Foundation for the Worldwide Mission Mandate: Contemporary Missiology—An Introduction." *Perspectives on the World Christian Movement*, 4th Edition. Pasadena, William Carey Library, 2009.

Carlisle, Thomas. *You! Jonah!* Grand Rapids, Eerdmans, 1968.

Introduction

God's Missionary Assignment for Israel

Israel: Blessed To Be A Blessing

Centuries before the time of the Old Testament prophets, God spoke to Abraham, the Father of all the faithful, saying, "In you shall *all the nations of the world be blessed*." This statement left no doubt—God's plan for mankind's redemption included every nation. Although God chose to work through the nation of Israel, He never intended that Israel alone be the exclusive recipient of His mercy and salvation. He did not choose Israel because the nation was extraordinary. He chose her that she might become the nation of missionaries to the world—His missionaries proclaiming the exclusivity of the only true God, the Most High God. He chose Israel as the peculiar nation among all the nations to keep His laws and model His character, and worship Him alone before a watching world. He chose Israel as His own to show the world His patient love and compassion for all people without respect to creed, color or ethnicity. The nation of Israel was chosen to carry God's light and become the means of blessing the entire world as she faithfully embodied the character of her God—the Most High God. Israel was blessed by God to be a blessing.

Rebellion: The Tragedy Of Israel, God's People

Under strong God-ordained leadership, Israel followed the ways of God and experienced His promised blessings, but with time and the successive reigns of her many ungodly kings, the nation became tainted through idolatry and strayed from the path of God's righteousness. After King Solomon's reign, Israel divided into two separate kingdoms: the Northern Kingdom which retained the name "Israel" with Samaria as its capital, and the Southern Kingdom of Judah with Jerusalem as its capital.

As the nation experienced the hardship of division, the people of God completely abandoned their missionary mandate. Under the rule of 19 kings representing nine different families over a period of 208 years, the Northern Kingdom of Israel repeatedly defied the laws of God, and consequently weakened both nationally and spiritually only to be invaded, destroyed and captured by the Assyrians, the most powerful kingdom of the ancient world of that day.

Willfully abandoning the call of God to be His light to surrounding nations, Israel, the chosen people of the Most High God, became idolaters just like the world surrounding them. The gods of the Gentile nations slowly but surely replaced the one true and living God in the lives of His people. God's judgment arrived soon enough through the tragic captivity by the godless nation of Assyria—forever becoming a major milestone marking Israel's rebellious history. (See chart: Kings of the Northern Kingdom of Israel.)

Prophets: God's Provision For His People

In great mercy, however, God never allowed Israel to forget her missionary vision. In the midst of moral decline, there was an increasing need to remind her of her purpose; therefore, God sent prophets to warn of the certainty of judgment should they refuse to repent of their wickedness. God's love is universal and His concern is for all people. He is not willing for even one to perish. His intentions for salvation included heathen nations, giving them the opportunity to know Him and receive His saving grace. Israel was to function as His hands, His feet, His voice, His messenger to those lost in darkness. One by one, God raised up prophets to speak to His Israelite missionary nation. The prophets of God spoke faithfully both to the southern and northern kingdoms of the certain judgment to come. Israel's rebellious compromise was a serious matter to God. Her disobedience interfered with the purpose God intended for the world. How would the world know about His love and mercy apart from the voice of God's salvation made available to all?

> Romans 10:14–15: "But how will people call on Him whom they have not believed? And how will they believe in Him of whom they have not heard? And how will they hear without a preacher (messenger)? And how will they preach unless they are commissioned and sent for that purpose? Just as it is written and forever remains written, *'How beautiful are the feet of those who bring good news of good things!'*"

In the mysterious providence of a holy God, He chose to use ordinary men and women as His mouthpiece. The message of the Old Testament prophets was never easy to deliver and more difficult to digest, but God was nevertheless depending upon His people to remember their mission to the world. The sad truth, however, was clearly apparent. Instead of living as a holy people, set apart from the world, God's people became assimilated into it, losing their uniqueness as those "set apart" for the Most High God. Instead of allowing the light of God to shine through them, they allowed the darkness of the world to overcome them.

Because the light of God was no longer shining in the lives of His people, the assignments from God to His prophets were always difficult. Human beings have a strong bent toward stubbornness, independence and complacency. With the Northern Kingdom particularly, the people of God ignored the prophet's message and chose to remain comfortable in their idolatry and rebellion. They refused to believe or heed the sobering message coming to them from God through the voices of His prophets. God's call to obedience through His prophets, however, was uncompromising.

For those who chose to side step His commands, grave consequences followed. Thus, in God's perfect timing, the Northern Kingdom of Israel became ripe for God's judgment, and this judgment came in the form of the Assyrian captivity and loss of the Northern Kingdom.

Israel's Decline: Final Years of the Northern Kingdom

Before the actual captivity took place, there were prosperous times in the Northern Kingdom of Israel—at least from the way things appeared outwardly. It is entirely possible to look fine and healthy on the outside, while disease and death are slowly eating away at one's health from the inside. Such was the situation in the Northern Kingdom. The first half of the eighth century BC was a prosperous time. With economic prosperity comes apathy, pleasure and self-sufficiency. Before the 41-year reign of Jeroboam II, the Northern Kingdom's 13th king (790–749 BC), Israel's northern neighbor Damascus had steadily encroached upon Israel's borders. However, when the nation of Assyria subdued the Syrian city of Damascus in 797 BC, Israel's borders were no longer under the pressure of encroachment, and the Northern Kingdom under the rule of King Jeroboam, gradually reestablished its territory almost to the extent realized under King David and King Solomon. From all appearances, Israel *seemed* to be thriving with the favor of God. At the same time, infighting within the nation of Assyria had diminished her (Assyria's) appetite for conquering smaller nations like Israel. Thus, there was peace—a false peace.

This action on the part of Assyria reaffirmed the Israelites' sense that they were indeed the chosen people of God (Deuteronomy 32:10; Zechariah 2:8)—that God would surely take care of them, and that nothing could obviously happen to harm them. As a result of this presumption, the Israelites of the Northern Kingdom were lulled into a false sense of security mistakenly thinking that no matter what they did or how they lived, God would take care of them because they were "His special treasure"—His chosen people. Yet under the leadership of 19 successive ungodly kings, Israel forgot their God, and turned instead to heathen gods of wood and clay. During this time of Northern Kingdom prosperity, Amos and Hosea were two of God's prophetic voices warning the Northern Kingdom of impending judgment. Israel was severely testing God's patience.

Interestingly, in the midst of the prophets' messages to Israel, God had a message for the heathen nation of Assyria as well—and a most unexpected one at that! It was remarkably an offer of His grace to the cruel and godless people of Nineveh, the Assyrian capital city, but it was also a double-edged sword, for this message to Nineveh contained a warning of imminent judgment for her as well. If she should refuse the generous offer of God's gift of salvation, God's just judgment would also reckon with her. "God is the One who sets up kings and deposes them." He is the One who brings nations to power—not man! The prophetic messenger God chose to send to Nineveh with His offer of salvation was a most unlikely character and one in need of much spiritual "education." Somehow, this particular servant had much to learn about the mercy of the God he claimed to know and serve.

Jonah: God's Reluctant Prophet

Jonah's assignment was to take this "double-edged sword" message of love and mercy / wrath and judgment to the Assyrian people! But there was one huge problem. The one chosen for this unusual assignment loathed the Assyrians. He hated them with a passion—like every other patriotic Israelite. All of Israel feared these evil people and their unspeakable cruelty. Years of violence and brutality had left deep wounds in the Israelite psyche. Why would God want to forgive *them* (4:1)? It was beyond an Israelite's comprehension that the Most High God could even consider forgiveness and favor to these people! Thus, when the word of God came to Jonah, it was a prophetic word unlike any that had been heard before.

This calling from God was shocking because it was a call for a Hebrew prophet to leave his own people, Israel, and go out to a heathen

Gentile city. Up until this time in Israel's history, God's prophets had been sent only to God's wayward people—the people of the covenant. Jonah's mission, therefore, was unprecedented. Yet, it was this particular nation that was the object of God's missionary outreach.

There would have been no reason to send a warning to Nineveh through Jonah unless there was a chance of her judgment being averted. But why on earth would God want to help the most brutal enemies of His people? And if this was indeed God's mission, why choose Jonah— a man so full of hatred and bias? Everyone knew he was intensely patriotic and a highly partisan Hebrew nationalist. It was simply astounding that God's intention was to send a man like this to preach to the very people he most feared and hated. Nothing—absolutely nothing—about this mission made sense! How could a loving God ask anyone to betray his country's interests like this?

There is, however, a wideness in God's mercy! "God's ways are not our ways—neither are His thoughts our thoughts" (Isaiah 55:8). God was up to something *big*, and the key player in this unfolding drama was now to face the struggle of his life. Would he comply with an assignment he simply could not understand and refused to accept? If so, his understanding and his acceptance of God's great mercy would have to be radically altered!

There's a Wideness in God's Mercy

There is a wideness in God's mercy,
like the wideness of the sea.
There's a kindness in God's justice,
which is more than liberty.
There is no place where earth's sorrows
are more felt than up in heaven.
There is no place where earth's failings
have such kindly judgment given.

For the love of God is broader
than the measures of the mind.
And the heart of the Eternal
is most wonderfully kind.
If our love were but more faithful,
we would gladly trust God's word,
And our lives reflect thanksgiving for the goodness of our Lord.

Frederick William Faber[1]

Kings of Northern Kingdom, Israel[2]

King	Years of Reign	Dates B.C.	Biblical Reference
Jeroboam I	22	933—910	1 Kings 11:26—14:20
Nadab	2	910—909	I Kings 15:25—28
Baasha	24	909—886	I Kings 15:21—16:7
Elah	2	886—885	I Kings 16:6—14
Zimri	7 days	885	I Kings 16:9—20
Omri	12	885—874	I Kings 16:15—28
Ahab	22	874—853	I Kings 16:28—22:40
Ahaziah	2	853—852	I Kings 22:40
Jehoram (Joram)	12	852—841	2 Kings 3:1—9:25
Jehu	28	841—814	2 Kings 9:1—10:36
Jehoahaz	17	814—798	2 Kings 13:1—9
Jehoash	16	798—782	2 Kings 13:10—14:16
Jeroboam II	41	793—753	2 Kings 14:23—29
Zechariah	6 months	753	2 Kings 14:29—15:12
Shallum	1 month	752	2 Kings 15:10—15
Menahem	10	752—742	2 Kings 15:14—22
Pekahiah	2	742—740	2 Kings 15:22—26
Pekah	20	752—732	2 Kings 15:27—31
Hoshea	9	732—722	2 Kings 15:30—17:6

NOTES

1. Faber, Frederick William. "There's a Wideness in God's Mercy." 1862. Hymnary.org, https://hymnary.org/text/theres_a_wideness_in_gods_mercy. Accessed 27 February 2020.

2. Adapted from "Who Were the Kings of Israel and Judah." *Got Questions*, https://www.gotquestions.org/kings-Israel-Judah.html. Accessed 2 March 2020.

Story 1

Running From God

Jonah 1

Principle Truth:

God is willing to go to extreme measures
to eliminate pride and prejudice
in the hearts of his servants.

Key Concepts:

Doctrinal Truth: Missions
An Attribute of God: Compassion
Character Trait: Loving God through Surrender

Chapter 1

God Calls Jonah to Nineveh

*God is willing to go to extreme measures to eliminate
pride and prejudice in the hearts of His servants.*

"Now the word of the Lord came to Jonah, the son of Amittai
saying, 'Go to Nineveh, that great city, and proclaim judgment
against it, for their wickedness has come up before Me.'"
(Jonah 1:1-2)

On a day like all others, something significant occurred that changed the course of Jonah's life. God spoke! As clearly as the ring of a bell tone, God spoke. However, the message Jonah received was the last thing he wanted to hear! As an army general gives orders to his troops for battle, Jonah's marching orders included a direct word from Almighty God to go east to the city of Nineveh, the infamous capital city of the nation of Assyria and powerful enemy of Israel.

But, how could this be? There had to be some mistake! Jonah, therefore, ignored God's voice, turned in the opposite direction—toward Tarshish—and set into motion events he couldn't have dreamed of in his wildest imagination (1:3)! With one decision, like a massive earthquake that changes an entire landscape, the circumstances of Jonah's future were instantly altered. What might have been would never be, and what consequences were to follow could not be avoided!

For Jonah, no longer could the focus be primarily about Assyrian barbarians who desperately needed the truth of the Most High God. Jonah's story now became his own personal testimony of one who not only resisted God's assignment to reach these wayward people, but in fact, ran from it. Jonah did the exact opposite of what God clearly instructed—always a foolish and potentially deadly decision. He is a tragic but powerful study in what it looks like to disobey God's clearly revealed will. Called to go east, he went west. Directed to travel overland, he went to sea. Sent to the big city, he bought a one-way ticket to the opposite end of the known world!

Jonah's willful defiance spoke to a far greater disobedience than even the behavior of godless Assyrians to whom he was being sent; for to whom much is given, much is required. Jonah was an Israelite blessed with much. A strong believer in the Most High God and part of the covenant people of God, he knew the Holy Scriptures and the laws and commands of God. Therefore, for all the knowledge and advantage he had of Israel's God, he was responsible. Jonah, however, preferred his own choice of assignment rather than God's choice for him! These strange orders were unthinkable, and Jonah simply couldn't imagine himself in the midst of *these* people speaking to *them* about the love and goodness of *his God*—the Most High God. To Jonah, this assignment was inconceivable and even absurd.

Jonah concluded that because he could not see any good reason for God's orders, there weren't any. He doubted the wisdom and justice of his God, and we are often guilty of the same. We doubt that God is good, or that He is committed to our best interests; therefore, if we fail to see any good reason for something God says or directs us to do, we assume that there aren't any good reasons! It is deadly, however, to ignore the voice of God. It is also deadly when sin lies dormant and unaddressed in your life, for given the right circumstances, it will surely rise up and take hold. It is, therefore, a great blessing that God orchestrates the events of our lives to reveal what lies long hidden in our hearts. As James 1:2–3 states: "Consider it nothing but joy, my brothers and sisters, whenever you fall into various trials. Be assured that the testing of your faith produces endurance—leading to spiritual maturity and inner peace."

God's message to Jonah awakened a deeply rooted pride and prejudice in his heart, and because these sinful attitudes had become so much a part of him, fear, hatred, and ultimately rebellion against God's plan became his driving force. No longer could he hear the clear, unquestionable guidance of the word of the Lord. His prideful heart forbade it! Sin in the heart blocks the Spirit's guidance and prevents His empowering to accomplish the task. Therefore, Jonah took matters into his own hands and attempted to do the impossible—to run away from God. Like the hound of heaven, however, God in mercy, pursued him. *God is willing to go to extreme measures to eliminate pride and prejudice in the hearts of His servants.*

> Sin in the heart blocks the Spirit's guidance and prevents His empowering to accomplish the task.

In spite of selfish choices, God's grand missionary purpose was unfolding with perfect precision, and His purpose included a witness of His mercy and grace to be offered to the Ninevites—either with Jonah or without him! Regardless of Jonah's reluctance to fulfill the assignment, his life experiences including his foolish decisions were used by God to fulfill His mysterious plan to reach the Assyrians with His light and love. For Jonah's prophetic ministry to move forward, radical intervention would be the prescription. Essentially he wanted a God of his own making, a God who simply wiped out the bad people—the wicked Ninevites—and blessed the good people—including, of course, himself and his Israelite countrymen. Such a short-sighted perspective for a genuine servant of God must be corrected; otherwise, there can be no spiritual success and certainly no impact for greater kingdom causes.

The Most High God—not Jonah's perception of Him—continued

in merciful pursuit to show up, and Jonah would be thrust time and again into great fury and despair over a God whose ways he simply could not understand and refused to accept. To Jonah, a God of mercy toward such vile sinners was puzzling to say the least. He simply could not reconcile the mercy of God with the required justice of God in regard to the sinful lifestyle and wicked ways of the Assyrians. Just how could the Most High God be both just and merciful at the same time? Jonah could not reconcile the two opposing concepts.

As it is with all passages of the Bible, there is something far greater going on in Jonah's story that points the astute reader directly to the gospel and to God's son, Jesus Christ, who would be born as a baby in Bethlehem centuries later in God's precise timing, and who also would be sent to the lost and hopeless lot of sinful humanity with His free offer of salvation. Because Jesus Christ died on the cross for our sins, God can be infinitely just because all the sin of all humanity was punished there. The cross of Christ also explains how God can be infinitely merciful as well because He took our sin onto Himself. He paid for it by substituting Himself for us.

Jonah's experience compels us to look ahead at how God would one day save mankind though the One who called himself "the ultimate Jonah." Matthew 12:41 declares in Jesus' own prophetic words: "The men of Nineveh will stand up (as witnesses) at the judgment against this generation (the religious generation of Jesus' day), and will condemn it because they (the Ninevites) repented at the preaching of Jonah; and now, something greater than Jonah (Christ himself) is here." *Jesus Christ* did this so that He could be *both just (the Just) and the justifier (the Merciful)* of those who believe. Romans 3:26 states: "It was to demonstrate His righteousness at the present time, so that *He would be just and the One who justifies* those who have faith in Jesus and rely confidently on Him as Savior."

Jonah's story, therefore, is a precursor—a foreshadowing of God's greater story when He sent His only son into this lost world to bring not only justice, but mercy through salvation and deliverance from sin. As 2 Corinthians 5:21 states: "He (God) made Christ who knew no sin (the Just One) to be sin on our behalf, so that in Him we would become the righteousness of God" (that is, we would be made acceptable to Him and placed in a right relationship with Him by His gracious loving-kindness and mercy).

On the cross, the justice of God required full punishment for sin but in the same moment, the cross provided salvation freely to all who simply believe. On the cross, therefore, both the justice and the mercy of God fully cooperated and shone forth brilliantly with absolutely no contradiction. As Martin Luther said: When a Christian believes in the finished work of Christ, he or she is simultaneously made righteous in God's sight (justified) and yet still a sinner (but mercifully delivered from the power of sin). In Nineveh, God's intention was to offer this same potent formula of the application of His justice and mercy to the most godless sinners on earth at that time. It is the only thing both then and now that can transform an individual—the only thing capable of bringing reformation to an individual and to a nation.

So, one ordinary day, a most significant event happened in Jonah's life. God spoke! "The voice of God came to His chosen prophet Jonah, the son of Amittai saying, 'Arise, go to Nineveh, that great city, and proclaim against her, for their evil has come up before my face.' . . . *but Jonah arose to flee* to Tarshish . . . *away from the face of the Lord."*

GOING DEEPER

THE DOCTRINE OF MISSIONS

A Definition

Believers in Jesus must understand the foundation upon which the great commission of God to every Christian rests. We must comprehend the greater purposes of God and His mission for every believer. Only then shall we be able to persevere in the missionary task before us, with courage and humility, in spite of the world's misunderstanding, opposition and persecution. Has God revealed in Scripture that "mission" is His will for His people? Absolutely! Has God also revealed through His word that "mission" is His heart? Absolutely! Therefore, in reality it becomes a practical matter of simple obedience to the same voice of God that spoke to Jonah, whatever others may think or say. The Bible declares five things about a God who is "on mission" to bring His light and salvation into the darkness of the world.

1. The Most High God is the God of History.

If we have received the blessings of justification by faith, acceptance with God, and the indwelling Spirit of God, then *we* are beneficiaries today of the promises made to Abraham four thousand years ago. *History* is *His* story! *We are included in His story!* His story is the story of redemption and salvation, and every believer is to be a participant in this great kingdom enterprise of the saving of souls.

2. The Most High God is the God of the Covenant.

God is gracious enough to make promises, and He always keeps the promises He makes. All God's promises are true, but they are inherited "through faith and patience" (Hebrews 6:12). We must be content to wait for God's perfect timing as we await the fulfillment of His promises.

3. The Most High God is the God of Blessing.

"I will bless you," He said to Abraham (Genesis 12:2). God's attitude to His people is positive, constructive and enriching. Judgment, on the other hand, is His "strange work" (Isaiah 28:21). His principle and characteristic work is to bless *all people* with the gospel and salvation. This is His mission, and this must become ours as well. *We are blessed in order to be a blessing!*

4. The Most High God is the God of Mercy.

Revelation 7:9 states that the company of the redeemed in heaven will be "a great multitude which no man could number." The Bible teaches that the redeemed will somehow be an international throng so immense as to be countless. God's promise will be fulfilled, and Abraham's seed will indeed be as innumerable as the dust of the earth, the stars of the sky, and the sand on the seashore. All people, tribes and tongues are to be a part of this great throng.

5. The Most High God is the God of Mission.

God has promised to bless "all the families of the earth," and He has promised to do so "through Abraham's seed" (Genesis 12:3). *We are Abraham's seed by faith* and, therefore, the earth's families will be blessed *only if we go* to them with the message of the gospel. This is God's plan and His plain purpose, and this is the believer's mission. Our mission is to *go*! The significant phrase "all the families of the earth" must be written on our hearts if God's missionary purposes are to be fulfilled in the world today. It is this expression more than any other that reveals the living God of the Bible to be a missionary God.

It is this expression also which condemns all our pettiness and narrow-mindedness, our racial pride, our condescending attitudes, and our arrogant quest for power. We dare not adopt a hostile or scornful or even an indifferent attitude to any person of another color or culture if our God is indeed the God of "*all the families of the earth!*" We must become global Christians with a

> We must become global Christians with a global vision, for we serve a global God.

global vision, for we serve a global God. We must never forget God's 4000-year-old promise to Abraham: "By you and your descendants *all the nations of the earth* shall be blessed. We must be intentional about sharing this good news of the gospel—for this is our mission and this is God's heart![1]

Mission is Propelled by Passion for the Glory of God

With mission there must be passion—a passion that reflects the heart of a merciful Father for all the nations. Passion means whatever a person is willing to suffer for. The root meaning of the word "passion" comes from the Latin word, "paserre"—to suffer. It is that which you hunger for so intensely that you will sacrifice anything to have it. The word "apostle" means a sent one, a messenger. Our mission, therefore, is to be "passionate messengers" of the good news of the gospel. There must be a deliberate intentional choice to live with a passion for the worship of Jesus in the nations. We must be committed to the point of death to spreading His glory. It is the quality of those who are on fire for Jesus, who dream of the whole earth being covered with the glory of the Lord as the waters cover the sea (Habakkuk 2:14). It is the quality of those who wake up every day to see "all the families of the earth" *included* in that great throng in heaven mentioned in Revelation 7.

The Test for Mission-Focused Passion

How does one determine that passion for God's mission is present? Perhaps the best way to determine its presence is to look for its absence. Floyd McClung, Director of All Nations Institute and author of the book *Follow*[2] states: "I know when apostolic passion has died in my heart. It happens when I don't spend my quiet time dreaming of the time when Jesus will be worshiped in languages that aren't yet heard in heaven. I know it is missing from my life when I sing about heaven but live as if earth is my home. Passion for God's mission is dead in my heart when I dream more about sports, toys, places to go, and people to see, than I do about the nations worshiping Jesus."[3]

Those who have this kind of passion are planning to go, but willing to stay. Those who have lost it are those who make decisions based on the danger involved, not the glory God will get. You have it when you are deeply disappointed that God has not called you to leave your home and get out among those who have never heard His name. If you say you will do anything for Jesus, but you aren't willing to take risks and suffer for Him—then you aren't really passionate about Him, His purposes for both you and the world, or His mission.

The Example of Paul

Paul says in Romans 15 that it is his ambition—his passion—to make Christ known. It began for him with a revelation of Jesus that he nurtured all his adult life. After his encounter on the Damascus Road, knowing Jesus and making Him known consumed the remainder of Paul's life. He "gloried in Christ Jesus in his service to God" (Romans 15:17). By comparison, everything else was dung, garbage, stinking refuse. His ambition was born from his understanding that God longed for His Son to be glorified in the nations—that the "Gentiles might become an offering acceptable to God, sanctified by the Holy Spirit" (Romans 15:16).

Human enthusiasm cannot sustain the missionary's passion. It is God's passion we must have. When God invests His own passion in you—the desire to see His name glorified among all people—you simply must build and develop what God has given you. You must answer the call to go—you must fulfill the desires of God's heart! There is no genuine fulfillment, satisfaction or meaning apart from your direct involvement in His heart's passion for the world.

Four Criteria For Mission-Focused Passion

1. Abandonment to God

Too many people want the fruit of Paul's ministry without paying the price that Paul paid. He died. He died to everything. He died daily. He was crucified with Christ. This strong-willed, opinionated man knew that he must die to self. We live in a world of competing passions. It is possible to deceive ourselves into thinking we have biblical passion when, in reality, all we have done is to baptize the values of our culture and give them Christian names. We will have chosen missionary passion only when our hearts are filled with God's desire for his Son to be worshiped in all the nations. May we pray that God will be ruthless with us in revealing our selfish ambition and lack of willingness to die to ourselves. *He answers that prayer every time!*

2. Focus of Priority

The greatest enemy of the ambition to see Jesus worshiped in the nations is a lack of focus. Activity—even good works—without the desire that God's message be shared among all people is just activity—not missions. You can expend energy on all sorts of good things and not get one step closer to God's heart for the nations. The church has a calling and mission for which we must be passionate. God has called us to the nations, and we must focus on that as our priority, or we will not obey.

3. Strategic Prayer

You and I cannot expect to hear "Well done, good and faithful servant" based upon one minute conversations with God and shallow communication with the Master we claim to love and serve. And we certainly can't make it on that kind of prayer life in the darkest places of the world where Jesus is not yet known or worshiped. The darkness is far too dark and the forces of evil too strong! Only prayer can break the strongholds. We must learn to pray as Paul models for us. Paul himself said that he prayed "night and day . . . with tears . . . without ceasing . . . with thankfulness . . . in the Spirit . . . constantly . . . boldly . . . for godly sorrow . . . against the evil one." God's mission cannot be accomplished apart from strategic prayer.

4. Strategic Vision

If you live without a vision of the glory of God filling the whole earth, you are in danger of serving your own dreams of greatness as you wait to do "the next thing" God tells you. There are too many over-fed, under-motivated believers hiding behind the excuse, "God has not spoken to me." They are waiting to hear voices or see dreams—all the while living to make money, provide for their future, dress well and have fun. Paul was guided by one primary passion—the passion of God's heart for the lost. Acts 20 and 21 tell of his determination to go to Jerusalem despite his own personal anticipation of suffering, the warnings of true prophets, and the disapproval of his friends. Why did he go anyway? He had a revelation from God and a vision of a far greater priority than anything which concerned himself or his safety. His was one of greater motivation, greater passion, greater purpose—the glory of God. It was God's passion that the gospel be shared among the Gentiles—this is what mattered to Paul. Truly, his life is an example of God's missionary heart becoming his heart's passion.

The Most Dangerous People in the World

If you have mission-focused passion, you are, in the eyes of Satan, one of the most dangerous people on the planet. The world no longer rules your heart. You are no longer seduced by getting and gaining, but devoted to spreading and proclaiming the glory of God in the nations. You live as a pilgrim, unattached to the cares of this world. You are not afraid of loss. You even dare to believe you may be given the privilege of dying to spread His fame on the earth. The

> May we pray that God will be ruthless with us in revealing our selfish ambition and lack of willingness to die to ourselves.

Father's passions have become your passions. You find your satisfaction and your significance in Him. You are sold out to God and you live only for Him. Satan fears you, and the angels applaud you.

Your greatest dream is that His name will be praised in languages never before heard in heaven. Romans 15:20–21 was Paul's vision: "Accordingly I set a goal to preach the gospel, not where Christ's name was already known, so that I would not build on another man's foundation but instead I would act on this goal as it is written in Scripture, 'They who had no news of Him shall see, and they who have not heard of Him shall understand.'" Your reward is the look of pure delight that you anticipate seeing in His eyes when you finally see Him face to face. Everything you will ever sacrifice here will be more than worth it there as you rest from your labor in His glory forever.

> You can expend energy on all sorts of good things and not get one step closer to God's heart for the nations.

Jonah: God's Reluctant Missionary

Jonah lacked missionary passion. He was too full of pride and prejudice issues to realize just how great the mercy of God is. He had much to learn before the alignment between his heart and God's heart could come into proper balance. God's power in Jonah's life to accomplish the task before him was limited and blocked to the prospect of even minimal success. Even at the outset, it is easy to see in this reluctant prophet just how far from God he really was and how much heartache accompanies such a dangerous distance. It would take nothing less than an inexplicable near-death experience to humble Jonah's heart before a just and merciful God, and even then, Jonah's pride refused to be broken. How ironic that the very mercy God so desired to extend to the Ninevites was the same mercy Jonah so desperately needed himself! And wonder of wonders, God's will was to extend it to both! Freely! Lavishly!

PAUSE TO PONDER

Principles for Godly Living
Missions

1. It is deadly to ignore the voice of the Most High God.
2. The Most High God's love is universal, and His concern is for all people. He desires that no one perish.
3. When the Most High God calls, obedience is not an option. God's instructions are not negotiable.
4. The earth's families will be blessed *only if we go* to them with the message of the gospel.
5. We must become global Christians with a global vision, for we serve a global God.
6. We must be committed to the point of death to spreading His glory.
7. If you have mission-focused passion, you are, in the eyes of Satan, one of the most dangerous people on the planet.

Questions for Life Application

1. Recall a time when God called you to be His voice to a person, place or situation that was repulsive to you. What was your response?
2. Our God is a missionary God and has invited us to join Him where He is working. How are you currently "on mision" in your own family, in your workplace, or in other relationships?

NOTES

1. Stott, John R. W. "The Living God is a Missionary God." *Perspectives on the World Christian Movement*. 4th ed. Pasadena, William Carey Library, 2009.

2. McClung, Floyd. *Follow*. Colorado Springs, David C. Cook, 2010.

3. McClung, Floyd. "Apostolic Passion." *Perspectives on World Christian Movement*. 4th ed. Pasadena, William Carey Library, 2009.

Chapter 2

The Depravity of Nineveh and a Prophet's Heart

God is willing to go to extreme measures to eliminate pride and prejudice in the hearts of His servants.

When God calls, obedience is not optional. We disobey at great risk to both ourselves and to the great numbers of those who depend upon our witness. Countless souls perish because there is no witness. "How will they hear without a preacher?" (Romans 10:14). Nevertheless, Jonah was adamantly opposed to God's purpose for Nineveh. Surely He had made a mistake in selecting Assyria for salvation and Jonah as His messenger. He wrestled tirelessly within his soul to embrace this call of God upon his life. From any human perspective and for very good reason, his concerns were indeed valid. Our concerns, however, do not negate the commands of God.

The nation of Assyria had risen to extraordinary power upon the world stage and was noted particularly for its cruelty. Its history is as gory and blood-curdling as any history we know. In today's context, these people would be considered terrorists and Assyria, the "terrorist" state. Yet, this nation was now remarkably chosen by God as the object of missionary outreach!

The empire began demanding heavy tribute from Israel during the Northern Kingdom's reign of King Jehu (843–815 BC, whose time in power came mid-way into the lifespan of the Northern Kingdom's existence). Assyria's power threatened the Jewish Northern Kingdom throughout the lifetime of Jonah (the time of King Jeroboam II: 825–773 BC), building within him a growing hatred for the abuse and exploitation suffered by his people. After years of torment, in 722 BC, Assyria finally invaded and destroyed the Northern Kingdom and its capital, Samaria, assimilating Israelites there into their godless culture and producing what we know as "Samaritans"—despised by Jews as half-breeds for centuries to come.

Thus, the hatred and fear of the Assyrian people was not without good reason. The tactics they employed in conquering an enemy nation were ruthless. The usual procedure was to burn the city, mutilate all grown male prisoners by cutting off their hands and ears and gouging out their eyes. After this torture, the mutilated bodies were piled into a great heap to perish in agony from the brutal heat of the sun, flies, infected wounds, or by the victim's eventual suffocation. Even children were burned alive at the stake, while the chief of the conquered nation was routinely carried off to Assyria's capital city to be flayed alive for the king's amusement.

Our concerns do not negate the commands of God.

The motive behind this bizarre punishment was to produce such terror in the people conquered that they would submit without a fight. It was the king's delight to watch his servants use their bare hands to pull out people's tongues! Often a subject was bound by ropes, chained, placed on the ground and skinned alive. The mere mention of the nation's name conjured up paralyzing fear in the heart of every rational thinking Israelite. Surely God could have nothing but the most severe judgment and wrath for these unusually vile people. But God's ways are not our ways! Neither are His thoughts our thoughts!

Therefore, when God spoke to Jonah, "Arise, Jonah, and go to Nineveh," Jonah simply could not believe what he heard! Even God Himself declared the wickedness of the Assyrian people to be unprecedented. In His own words He expressed it precisely, ". . . their wickedness stinks to the heavens." Nevertheless, Jonah was to be God's voice in this wretched place whether he liked it or not! This assignment was not about what he loved or hated, or what was comfortable or easy. This was about God's greater purposes being fulfilled and Jonah, strangely enough, was God's choice to fulfill the mission.

The capital city with its 600,000 inhabitants was a huge megalopolis filled with massive fortifications. Because the people were quite superstitious, the evidence of idols to every heathen god and goddess could be witnessed everywhere. There was no respect for the sanctity of human life. Assyria was a culture of death. Jonah was to preach God's message of repentance and salvation to these barbarians. His assignment was to cry out against them, expose their unspeakable depravity and wretched way of living, and warn them that they had 40 days to turn from their evil ways. Should they refuse, they would be destroyed through the righteous justice of the Most High God!

To Jonah, the assignment itself appeared to be as cruel as the very people to whom he was being sent! These people didn't deserve the slightest favor from a holy God. To Jonah, this was a death sentence and a set-up for ultimate failure. Surely there was another way. Certainly God had a "Plan B" that would suit this reluctant prophet at least a little better than this perplexing instruction! Jonah began recalculating his options. Disregarding what he had so clearly heard, Jonah ran. He ran from the voice of God. He ran from His calling. He ran from the Most High God.

But, wait. It is impossible to run from God, for God sees all and knows all and is ever present. He is everywhere at once! In his prideful rebellion Jonah was cruelly deceived, and such deception always comes at a high cost!

"Where can I go from your Spirit? Where can I flee from your presence? If I go up to the heavens, you are there; if I make my bed in the depths, you are there." (Psalm 139:7–8)

Jonah's disobedience was pointless. He was soon to be "found" by this God of mercy and undeserved second chances. *God is willing to go to extreme measures to eliminate pride and prejudice in the hearts of His servants.*

Jonah's disobedience led to his being deceived which consequently exposed the rebellion lying long dormant in his heart. The deception was subtle at first and came in the form of a set of perfectly aligned circumstances that were easily misinterpreted. Ironically, there was a ship waiting in the harbor of Joppa at the very moment Jonah arrived; therefore, he surmised,

"This must be God's will because the ship is sailing to the very location I am going—Tarshish—and is sitting right here waiting for me to board! What a coincidence!! There is no public schedule of ships here at the port; therefore, for a ship to be in port waiting right here in the harbor at the exact time I arrived here—going to the precise location I want to go—well, this *must* be from God!"

Make no mistake! There will always be a "ship" of some sort waiting to take you away from the will of the Most High God. The enemy of our souls is quite clever and his most powerful tool is deception. Once we determine what we are going to do, we can always interpret the circumstances any way we wish. Jonah had deliberately decided on his own exactly what he was going to do. He had taken a 75-mile journey from his home to Joppa to prove that point, and he now began the deadly task of interpreting his circumstances in order to rationalize his own personal determination. God, however, instructs us to "Trust in the Lord with all your heart and lean not to your own understanding. In all your ways acknowledge Him and He will direct your path" (Proverbs 3:5).

But not only was there a ship in the harbor waiting to transport him to Tarshish, as he reached into his pocket, he found that miraculously the exact amount of money for the fare was right there as well!

"My goodness! I have precisely the amount of money I need to reach the city of Tarshish; indeed, this trip has to be divinely ordained of God—this *must* be of God! The ship is here, the money is here, this is proof that my decision is the right one! A voyage to Tarshish—that's exactly what I will do!"

But the Most High God had spoken—*clearly*. He had not changed His mind! There was no inconsistency about His guidance. Jonah's assignment was Nineveh; for God had purposes in mind of which Jonah knew nothing. Jonah was to be God's mouthpiece to a specific place, at a specific time, to a specific people. Admittedly, there were mysterious "coincidences" that appeared to be unmistakable evidence of God's guidance, but besides all that, there was the nagging truth Jonah knew with certainty deep in his heart. He had clearly heard the voice of God. He knew the will of God for his life! God has certain standards that are absolutely clear, and we must not orchestrate our circumstances to rationalize our less than best choices. If we have a clear word from God, we must never interpret our circumstances to support any action other than unwavering obedience to that word. The will of God is always revealed through the word of God. The two are inseparable and always consistent.

> Once we determine what we are going to do, we can always interpret the circumstances any way we wish.

Jonah was cruelly deceived in his disobedience. He wandered down the dangerous path of self-deception—the Main Street of Satan's wicked schemes. We are wise to heed the lessons of his negative example. When we decide to disregard God and take matters into our own hands, the world will always have a "ship" waiting to take us where we want to go. And we will often have the exact amount of money to make the trip! Jonah failed to realize at this point that his refusal to heed God's command would result in the greatest storm of his life! Every act of disobedience to God has a storm attached to it!

Nevertheless, storms are used by God for our good. The greatest danger is that we never become aware of our blindness, pride and self-sufficiency. Unfortunately, we believe falsely that we have far more ability to direct our lives wisely than we really have, and that we are far more virtuous, honest and decent than we really are. These are deadly errors of self-judgment, and Satan is happy to allow us to indulge those thoughts and enjoy our prideful, pleasant, and prosperous life for many years so that we never see the truth until it is too late. Out of His great mercy, however, God awakens us to the true condition of our heart, and in many lives, He uses storms to do it. There is undeserved mercy at the heart of our storms for our God is full of love and compassion!

> Every act of disobedience to God has a storm attached to it!

GOING DEEPER

ATTRIBUTE OF GOD: COMPASSION

A Definition

Compassion: emotions and feelings about someone's difficulty or misfortune; the capacity for sharing the painful feelings of another. Compassion implies pity coupled with an urgent desire to aid or to spare. Compassion refers to both a feeling and the action that stems from that feeling. Compassion is the inward urging to reach out in love to those around us who are in need.[1]

The Radical Compassion of God

Throughout the Bible and the history of God's people, the compassionate nature of God was extended freely to poor, wandering, lost sinners—Jew and Gentile alike—and is one of the most compelling attributes of God's revelation of Himself to mankind. God knows the extent of depravity and evil of which every human being is capable. Yet this does not exhaust God's love and patience. As astounding as it seems, He continues to take His rebellious children by the hand. His arms are always open to the return of prodigals, for His compassion and His mercies never fail.

"It is because of the Lord's loving-kindness that we are not consumed, because His tender compassions never fail. They are new every morning; great and beyond measure is Your faithfulness." (Lamentations 3:22–23)

The Shocking "Attachment" of God to His Children

Ancient philosophers were known for speaking of "the love of benevolence" which meant doing good and helpful things for people even if you did not have affection for them. Love of benevolence was an exercise of the will. It meant performing loving actions even if your heart was not drawn to affection for someone. In contrast, according to the philosophers, there was also the "love of attachment" in which you loved someone because your heart was bound up with them in attraction and loving desire. The Greek Stoic philosophers insisted that God was marked by "apatheia"—a Greek word from which we get our English word "apathy" (indifference; detached). Their thinking was that God could certainly do loving things, but "a god" was elevated far above human status and could not possibly demean Himself by having a heart attachment to mere human beings so far beneath their status. That is why God's language in the Bible about Himself is no less than shocking. The word for "compassion" used in the final chapter of Jonah 4:10–11 is a word that means to grieve over someone or something, to have your heart broken, to weep for it.

After all of Jonah's life-changing experiences, it was necessary for God to continue showing the prophet his wicked heart—still in desperate need of cleansing. Finally, after Jonah reluctantly preached in Nineveh (Jonah

3) through the mercy of the God of second chances, he went outside the city to pout. God graciously provided a plant to miraculously grow up to provide him shade, then just as quickly, God sent a worm to destroy the plant. Once more, Jonah was furious and resorted to what was so natural for him—pouting. God said to Jonah, "You had compassion for the plant" (4:10). That is, God says, "You wept over it, Jonah. Your heart became "attached" to it. When it died, it grieved you." Then God says, in essence, "*You* weep over plants, but *my compassion* is for *people.*" For God to apply this particular word to Himself is radical, for this is the language of attachment. God weeps over the evil and lost condition of the Ninevites. He is not detached from their hopeless state—He is not apathetic.

When you attach your love upon someone, you can be happy only if they are happy, and their distress becomes your distress. The love of attachment, however, makes you vulnerable to suffering. And *yet* that is precisely what God says of Himself in Jonah 4 and in many other places of the Word of God. Isaiah 63:9 is another Old Testament example of God's attachment to His people: "In all their suffering He also suffered, and He personally rescued them. In His love and mercy He redeemed them. He lifted them up and *carried them* through all the years."

A Compassionate "Carrying" God[2]

Our compassionate God "carries" those for whom He cares. He is a "carrying" God, and at times we all need to be carried. We can be like little children who fall behind because our legs are too weak to keep walking. Other times, we might be more like lambs that persist in straying from the Shepherd and risk falling prey to enemies. Our God promises to carry us—even until our old age (Isaiah 46:4). But it costs to carry. In order for Jesus to carry our sins, He first had to carry His cross—but in mercy, He carried that cross for us. Likewise, we reflect His likeness by carrying one another's burdens. It costs to carry, but we only need to think of Jesus' example and thank Him for never getting tired of carrying us.

God's compassion is on display as well in Genesis 6:6 where we are told that when God looked down on the evil of the earth, "His heart was filled with pain." While this language cannot mean that the eternal unchangeable God loses any of His omnipotence or sovereignty, it is nevertheless, a strong declaration at which we must marvel! This thought becomes even more profound as we consider the fact that human beings need many things, and we get emotionally attached to things that meet those needs. God, however, needs nothing. He is utterly and perfectly happy in Himself, and He doesn't need us. So how could He get attached to us? The only answer to this question is that an infinite, omnipotent, self-sufficient divine being loves voluntarily, unconditionally. How could God say, "What happens to Nineveh affects Me. It moves Me. It grieves Me"? It simply means He voluntarily attaches His heart. Elsewhere, time and time again, we see God looking at Israel sinking into the mire of evil, sin and idolatry, and God speaks about His heart literally turning over within Him. "How can I give you up, O Ephraim? How can I hand you over, O Israel? . . . My heart recoils within me; my compassion grows warm and tender" (Hosea 11:8).

God's compassion is not something abstract but concrete. It plays out not just in His attitude but in His actions toward human beings. It is interesting that He speaks of these violent, sinful pagans as people "who do not know their right hand from their left" (Jonah 4:11). That is an exceedingly generous way to look at the people of Nineveh! It means that they were spiritually blind, hopeless and had lost their way. They haven't the first clue as to the source of their problems or what to do about them. Obviously, God's threat to destroy Nineveh shows that this blindness and ignorance is ultimately no excuse for the evil they had perpetrated, but it does show remarkable sympathy and understanding from a God of incredible compassion. It shows Nineveh's desperate need of a light in the darkness—for a voice of truth, for the knowledge of this loving, merciful and compassionate God who desires above all else that they too have opportunity to know Him.

The Compassion of God in the Person of Jesus Christ

By far the most typical statement of Jesus' emotional life was the phrase "He was moved with compassion," a Greek phrase that means He was moved from the depths of His being. The Bible records Jesus weeping 20 times for every one time it notes that He laughs. He was a man of sorrows, and not because He was naturally depressed. He had enormous joy in the Holy Spirit and in His Father, yet He grieved far more than He laughed because His compassion connected Him with us—attached His love to sinful human beings. Our sadness makes Him sad; our pain brings Him pain. He is the compassionate prophet Jonah should have been. But Jesus was infinitely more than Jonah. He did not merely weep for us; He died for us. Jonah went outside the city, hoping to witness not its repentance, but its condemnation; Jesus went outside the city of Jerusalem to die on a cross to accomplish our salvation. The contrast between the two is staggering.

The Parable of the Lost Sheep[3]

Perhaps the compassion of God is expressed most beautifully in Jesus' parables of the lost things recorded in the gospel of Luke. In the parable of the lost sheep, the shepherd never ceases to care for the sheep that did not go astray. They remain safe in the sheepfold, but there is a particular compassion actively on display for the one lost sheep that wandered away from the fold. Though he has a hundred sheep, a considerable flock, the shepherd refuses to lose even one, for every sheep is equally valued, loved and important. The shepherd knows each one by name and is attached to each sheep. The good shepherd goes after the one lost sheep showing an incredible abundance of loving care toward the one who is lost. He searches until he finds it. He then places the sheep upon his shoulders and returns it to the safety of the fold.

Likewise, God sent his only Son to seek and save that which was lost. Matthew 9:36–38 states: "When He (Jesus) saw the crowds, *He was moved with compassion* and pity for them, because they were dispirited and distressed, like sheep without a shepherd. Then He said to His disciples, 'The harvest is indeed plentiful, but the workers are few. So pray to the Lord of the harvest to send out workers into His harvest.'" The people of Nineveh were desperately lost—not just one of them but all of them! They were lost sheep without a shepherd. Just as the shepherd grieved over one lost sheep and went after it as if nothing else mattered, so God was deeply grieved over the condition of the lost people of Nineveh and was sending Jonah to them to share this same love and compassion.

God allowed the evil of that city to weigh on Him and in some mysterious way; He was suffering because of its sin. When God came into this world in Jesus Christ and went to the cross, He didn't experience only emotional pain, but every kind of pain in unimaginable dimensions. The agonizing physical pain of the crucifixion included torture, slow suffocation and excruciating death. Beyond that, when Jesus hung on the cross, He understood fully the infinite and most unfathomable pain of all—separation from God the Father, eternal alienation, and the agonizing weight of mankind's sin. He did it all for us, out of His unimaginable compassion. He came so that He might "carry us."

"He lifted them up and carried them through all the years." (Isaiah 63:9)

May we pray to be models of compassion and grace—reflections of the loving heart of our compassionate heavenly Father.

PAUSE TO PONDER

Principles for Godly Living
God's Compassion

1. Every act of disobedience has a storm attached to it; however, God's mercy can always be found in the storm for God is full of love and compassion.

2. Although God knows fully the extent of evil to which human beings are capable, His compassions are new each day.

3. God's arms are always open to the return of the prodigals, for His compassion and mercies never fail.

4. Every sheep (person) is equally valuable, loved and important.

5. Countless souls perish because there is no witness. God expects His servants to share His compassion with the lost.

Questions for Life Application

1. Share a time when you, like Jonah, ignored God's clearly revealed instructions. What "ship" took you away from the revealed will of God, and who was affected negatively by your disobedience?

2. In what areas of your life do you strive for something God has not yet given you or promised you? Where is your striving leading you? How does relying on your own efforts change how you view yourself and how you view God?

NOTES

1. Elwell, Walter A. and Philip W. Comfort. *Tyndale Bible Dictionary*. Carol Stream, Tyndale House Publishers, 2001.

2. Briscoe, Jill. "A Carrying God." *Telling the Truth Devotional*, May 29, 2019, https://www.ourdailydevotionals.com/2019/05/29/carried-one-year-devotions-for-women-2019/. Accesed 27 February 2020.

3. Bishop, Mary Ann. *Servants of the Most High God: Stories of Jesus, the Teaching Ministry and Parables.* Maitland, Xulon Press, 2016.

Chapter 3

The Storm of a Lifetime

---

*God is willing to go to extreme measures to eliminate
pride and prejudice in the hearts of His servants.*

With details in perfect order and the fare for the journey paid, Jonah boarded the ship bound for Tarshish—away from the revealed will of the Most High God. We always pay in full for riding the ships of the world for they take us away from God and are one-way journeys—*down*; that is, unless God, in compassion, intervenes to bring us back up some other way. *God is willing to go to extreme measures to eliminate pride and prejudice in the hearts of His servants.* Thus, Jonah's disobedience set into motion the deadly unraveling of the catastrophic events soon to unfold. He went *down* to Joppa, *down* into the ship, *down* into the deep, *down* into the belly of a great fish. The fish itself then went *down* into the depths of the sea. Make no mistake. When we walk away from the presence of the Lord, the journey will always be *down, down, down*.

Storms are often disguised gifts from God intended to show us who we really are! The uncovering of Jonah's heart was not a pleasant sight; however, "heart disease" must be diagnosed and treated before a cure can come. Storms wake us up to truths we would otherwise never see. Greater still is the fact that deep within the terror of the storm, God's mercy, whether we realize it or not, is always at work drawing us back to the only One capable of healing a diseased heart. The bigger issue at stake is not the storm itself, but what the storm exposes.

As the ship left the harbor and the shoreline of Joppa gradually grew faint in the distance, the sky began to darken. What started as a beautiful day now became ominous and foreboding. Everyone on board sensed it. There was just something "unexplainable"—unspoken—about the very atmosphere itself! Indeed, something of great significance was about to happen, and it had everything to do with the fulfillment of God's great redemptive purposes for the lost souls of Nineveh. Within only moments, the sea became angry with such turbulence that everyone on board realized this was no typical storm. It was indeed fast becoming a tempest of unprecedented power! *"The Most High God sent a great wind,"* as the sea rose like a huge wall so that the ship was tossed about like a toy and certain to break up. The Bible states that God *"hurled"* this great wind upon the sea—a vivid picture of the Lord God purposefully launching this mighty tempest directly at Jonah's boat.

The sailors were terrified and knew without question they would perish in the deep waters. These were experienced sailors who took bad weather in stride, but this storm was different—a uniquely terrifying monster! The sailors began to cry out to their various gods convinced that someone on board must have done something horrible for the gods to manifest such anger in this particular way. They struggled to steady the boat and meet the impossible demands of the ever-increasing waves crashing into them without mercy. They threw the cargo into the sea to lighten the ship. With the entire crew in crisis mode, the sailors did everything possible to stabilize their desperate situation. Remarkably, Jonah was sleeping like a baby, totally unaware of the great danger to which the ship and its crew were exposed. The sailors worked their fingers to the bone bailing the water. Even for seasoned sailors, the fear was overwhelming. The captain, fully aware of the certainty of death, went down to the sleeping prophet, shook him awake, and shouted above the roar of the mighty wind and waves,

"Man, how can you sleep? The gods are furious at us for some unknown reason! Get up and call on your God! Just maybe He will take notice of us and protect us from perishing."

How ironic! Jonah refused to talk to Ninevite heathens about God or lead them toward faith in the one true God—his God. So, he fled, only to find himself now talking about his God to the exact sort of people from whom he was fleeing! These sailors were spiritually astute enough to sense that this was not just a random storm. They were smart enough to conclude that the tempest was of divine origin, and quite possibly a response to someone's grave sin—*someone, no doubt, in the company of this boat.* They were not narrow-minded and bigoted. Incredibly, they were open to calling on Jonah's God. In fact, they were more ready to do so than was Jonah! How strange! Ironically, God sent His prophet to point pagans toward Himself, yet now it was the pagans who were pointing the prophet toward his God. Discerning that there was human sin and a divine hand behind these frightening events, the sailors cast lots, a practice quite common in ancient times to determine a guilty party. Unaware of the orchestrations of Almighty God in every detail, even the casting of lots was God's means of exposing Jonah's disobedience to the sailors in order to bring his guilt to light.

The sailors said to one another, "Come let us cast lots to find out who is responsible for this horrible calamity." And as they cast lots, the lot fell on Jonah! So they asked him, "Tell us, man, who is responsible for making all this trouble for us? What in the world have you done? Where did you come from? What is your country? From what people are you?"

The captain's words were a strong rebuke and spoke directly to Jonah's strange indifference of impending disaster common to them all. Obviously, Jonah had no interest whatsoever in their common good. How in the midst of deadly calamity, could the one responsible for it all be so oblivious to their needs? Why wasn't Jonah using his faith in his God for the good of all? It just didn't make sense! They were all in the same storm, subject to the same peril, and they would soon experience the same outcome. But Jonah's lack of concern reflected a deep-seated problem—deeper than was evident at the outset of the journey. He was running from God because he did not want to work for the good of pagans—he wanted to serve exclusively the interests of his own people. God, however, was showing him that He is the God of all people, and Jonah desperately needed to see himself as a part of the whole community of mankind—not simply a member of a certain exclusive faith community.

We are responsible for how we live. The world will not see who our Lord is if we do not live as we should. We deserve the harsh critique of the world if the body of Christ does not exhibit visible love in practical deeds. The captain had every right to rebuke this prophet of the living God who was oblivious to the problems of the people around him and who chose to do nothing for them. Jonah was a follower of the one true God. How was it possible that pagans were outshining him? Tragically, nonbelievers sometimes act more righteously than do believers, despite their lack of faith; whereas believers, unrepentant and filled with remaining sin, often act far worse than their "right belief" in God would lead us to expect. There are many good, moral people who are not believers in the Most High God. Lifestyle must match theology, or the message is at best compromised and at worst negated. Through Jonah's indifference and self-righteous arrogance, the truth was made known to all that he had no respect for those surrounding him in this tempest he himself had caused.

> We deserve the harsh critique of the world if the body of Christ does not exhibit visible love in practical deeds.

To the sailor's questions of his purpose, his place and his race, Jonah answered in a most telling way,

"I am a Hebrew, and I worship the Lord, the God of heaven,
the God who made the sea and the land."

This terrified the men; therefore, they asked Jonah,

"Well, what have you done?"

They knew that he was running from God because he had mentioned this earlier. The sailors knew also that identity is always rooted in the things to which we give our ultimate allegiance. For them to ask, "Who are you?" was essentially to ask, "Whose are you?" To know who you are is to know what you have given yourself to, what controls you, and what you most fundamentally trust. Jonah's order of identification was revealing. While he did have faith in God, it appears not to have been as fundamental to his identity as was his race and nationality—which he mentioned first. Obviously his relationship with the Most High God was not as basic to his significance as was his race. That is why when loyalty to his people and loyalty to the Word of God seemed to be in conflict, he chose to support his nation over taking God's love and message to a new people.[1]

This shallow misplaced perception of his identity prevented him from truly seeing himself as God saw him, and his future was now to take a dramatic turn in order for God to teach him the painful truth of just how far from God he truly was—although at this point he would never have admitted it! It was becoming all too clear. Jonah needed the mercy of God just as much as the godless Nin-

> Lifestyle must match theology, or the message is at best compromised and at worst negated.

evites did. The journey out of his deeply rooted self-righteousness, however, would prove to be a slow and painful one.

Time was running out and as the sea raged, the sailors pushed Jonah for a final solution. Now that they knew he was indeed the cause of their trouble, they reasoned as well that he was the key to solving their great dilemma.

"Tell us, Jonah, just what should we do to you to make the sea calm down for us?"

And Jonah answered,

"Pick me up and throw me into the sea, and it will become calm again. *I know* that this is my fault. I am the cause of this great storm that has come upon you."

Witnessing the sheer terror on the faces of these pagan sailors to whom he was speaking, something awakened in Jonah. These men had been calling on their pagan gods while he had not even spoken to his. They had questioned him respectfully, asking him what they should do rather than simply killing him. They were innocent men and had done nothing wrong at all. Obviously moved by their kindness, this was the first step in Jonah's coming to his senses. He actually began to think of someone other than himself—pagan sailors at that! Essentially he said to them: "You are dying for me, but I should be dying for you! I am the one with whom God is angry—*throw me into the sea*!"

Instead, the men did their best to row back to land. It quickly became obvious, however, that they could not, for the sea became even wilder than before. Then they all cried out in anguish to the Lord, the God of heaven—Jonah's God—the Most High God:

"O Lord, please do not let us die for taking this man's life. Do not hold us accountable for killing an innocent man, for You, O Lord, have done as you pleased."

Asking forgiveness for what they knew they must do, the sailors—out of sheer desperation—took Jonah and threw him overboard, and immediately the seas grew calm. At this miracle, the men greatly *feared the Lord*, and offered a sacrifice to the Most High God and made vows to Him. The impact of God's miraculous power upon the pagan sailors was profound. They realized instantly that Jonah's God is the God who made the sea and as such, controlled the seas. They were in awe at the majestic power they had witnessed and were "seized" with an even greater "fear" than when they thought they would surely drown. This was a new kind of fear—the fear the Bible refers to as the beginning of wisdom, the "fear of the Lord"—the Most High God, the one and only true and living God (Jonah 1:16). The sailors used the covenant name of the Most High God, "Yahweh," the Hebrew name that speaks of a personal saving relationship with this living God. The fear of the Lord is the essence of all saving knowledge and wisdom. Genuine salvation begins here.

The sailors initially thought of the Most High God as merely Jonah's tribal deity, but in light of what they had witnessed, they came face to face with the matchless power of who this God really was. People under duress often make vows to God when there is impending doom, but after the danger passes, the best of intentions fade away. These men were different. They made their vows *after* the danger passed—indicating that they were not seeking God for what He could do for them, but simply for who He had revealed Himself to be. This understanding of God—this fear of the Lord—was *their* beginning of true wisdom and genuine faith. How ironic! Jonah's reluctance to be God's missionary to Nineveh resulted in the conversion of non-Israelites—pagan sailors! What God purposes, He always performs! He uses everything and wastes nothing!

But the Most High God had not forgotten nor forsaken Jonah. He is the great Jehovah Jireh—the God who provides. With incredible compassion extended toward His wayward prophet, God sent a great fish to swallow and preserve Jonah. Jonah remained deep inside the belly of that fish for three days and three nights. At times God must go to great lengths to get the attention of a reluctant "servant." *God is willing to go to extreme measures to eliminate pride and prejudice in His servants.*

> What God purposes, He always performs! He uses everything and wastes nothing!

The Most High God is the Creator of all. He has power over all nature and all the elements of the universe. As such, He orchestrated the great storm to retrieve His disobedient prophet. Likewise, He orchestrated the great fish to save Jonah and in mercy gave him a second chance at getting things right! *When we run from God, we are always headed for a storm.* Jonah needed a storm to awaken him to the potentially fatal disease of his ever-hardening heart. God uses everything—even our disobedience and certainly our worst storms. As God dealt with Jonah, pagan sailors were providentially brought to saving faith in Jonah's God. The living God is forever working on multiple levels simultaneously. He orchestrates every detail in the circumstances of life.

Because God loved Jonah and had a specific plan for his life, He was determined to draw His servant back into His great redemptive purposes through His merciful pursuit. God determined from the beginning to redeem people from every tongue, tribe and nation. This missionary mandate is the steady heartbeat of our compassionate God, but He must have obedient servants to carry out His plans. Sadly, He was having quite a time with this particular one!

> God determined from the beginning to redeem people from every tongue, tribe, and nation.

GOING DEEPER

CHARACTER TRAIT: LOVING GOD THROUGH SURRENDER[2]

A Definition

Mark 12:30 is one of the most important statements Jesus ever spoke and provides in summary the criteria by which all genuine followers of Christ must live. In answer to the question asked by a scribe, one of the experts in Mosaic Law:

"Which commandment is first and most important of all?"

Jesus answered:

"The first and most important one is 'Hear, O Israel, the Lord our God is one Lord; and *you shall love the Lord your God* with all your heart, and with all your soul (life) and with all your mind (thought), and with all your strength.'"

According to Jesus, living one's life by this commandment is the distinguishing factor of those who claim to know and serve Christ. This is the first and most important commandment, but (according to Jesus) the second is like unto it: "Love your neighbor as yourself" (Matthew 22:39). No less than nine times is this commandment stated and restated in the Word of God. (Deuteronomy 6:5; 10:12; 11:13; 13:3; 30:6; Joshua 22:5; Matthew 22:37; Mark 12:30; Luke 10:27).

In Matthew 22:38, Jesus states in no uncertain terms that this is the "first and greatest commandment." Three words (first, greatest, commandment) underscore its importance. The words "first" and "greatest" together declare that loving God is indispensable, while the word "commandment" describes it as a non-negotiable part of our moral and ethical way of life. For something to be indispensable means there can be no life without it—it is indispensable to one's existence. It is this central reality from which all of life flows. "First" means that thing to which everything else is subsequent, dependent or secondary. "Greatest" means more important in rank or position. Loving God, therefore, is the center point, the starting point, and the ultimate priority of life; nothing is more essential to a life of righteousness, purpose and meaning. This command is an absolute statement to which the believer must conform.

Biblical righteousness does not begin with our preferences. God's righteousness is settled and authoritative. God does not change His standards to conform to us. His standards are the expression of what is right and our behavior becomes righteous as we come into alignment with them. Loving God, therefore, begins with understanding every word Jesus spoke in Matthew 22:38 (and other references cited above).

The Practical Expression of Loving God

What does the choice to love God entail? It means to give, to yield, to surrender to another. It begins with understanding the word for love (agape) Christ used in His teaching in the gospel accounts and particularly in Matthew 22:38. Significantly, "agape" is not primarily an emotional kind of love; God is not asking us to always feel good about Him. Agape love is not a feeling—it is a choice. God always directs His commands to our free will, not our emotions.

In his superb book, *Fan the Flame*, author Joe Stowell uses an excellent illustration of a "Yield" sign. When we drive down a highway, we often encounter "Yield" signs that encourage us to "give way" to the flow of traffic, to merge into the traffic with caution and care. In a sense, the will of God moves through the territory of a life like a major highway. His will is His eternal plan and program, with a specific place and specific principles for each life and each situation. He asks that I yield, that I "give way" to Him and that I merge my life into His will. His will intercepts my life.[3] Loving Him is practically expressed in my willingness to yield to Him, to His guidance, to His commands. Any attempt to ignore God's traffic "Yield" signs will result in the devastating consequences of sin.

As we lovingly yield to our Lord, we may be asked to yield our preferences, our pride, our passions, our desires, our dreams, our possessions, our time, our resources, and even our friends and family; yet loving God must be the ultimate priority. The Bible makes it clear that we love Him because He first loved us. We choose to love Him regardless of how we feel. Our love should not waver or become inconsistent because of vacillating feelings and emotions. Christ is declaring that the expression of true love for God—the way that we respond to the fact that He surrendered Himself to meet our sin problem—is to yield to Him as Lord and Master. Yielding my will for the sake of His will is the ultimate statement of how much I love Him. He does not want our words, our rituals or our habits. He wants us to love Him with our hearts, our souls, our minds, and with our choices. He wants us to prove to Him that He is truly worth more than anything else to us.

As we love God, we choose to lay the baggage of our selfish and sinful choices at the base of the "Yield" sign and then get caught up in the momentum of the flow of His good and perfect will for us—allowing Him to move in us and through us accomplishing His purposes. Yielding to God, therefore, is the tangible way for the follower of Christ to say, "I love you, Lord." Love looks for significant ways to prove itself. The significance of the gift, however, is not so much in the gift itself as it is in the thought that the gift expresses. Romans 6–8 describes vividly the strength of the flesh as we struggle in that process of yielding our will to God's will. Yielding to God's will involves struggle and most often an outright battle of wills. Our passion and pride can be a most powerful force. Naturally, we love ourselves more than we love our Savior. But surrendering to the will of God is the privileged response of the believer's love. Surrender—yielding—is the outward expression of our love of God. Paul's counsel in Romans 12:1–2 sums it up best:

> "Therefore, I urge you, brothers and sisters, by the mercies of God, to present your bodies (dedicating *all* of yourselves, set apart) as a living sacrifice, holy and well pleasing to God, which is your rational (logical, intelligent) act of worship. And do not be conformed to this world, but be transformed (and progressively change as you mature spiritually) by the renewing of your mind (focusing on godly values), so that you may prove for yourselves what the will of God is, that which is good and acceptable and perfect (in His plan and purpose for you)."

Six Dynamics at Work in the Believer's Surrender to God

1. Surrender is a choice.

If my heart is set on surrender, then I will choose to do what He calls me to do. This is the proof of my love of God. When faced with a decision in life, I must begin by asking, "What would it mean for me to surrender to God at this time?" The answer to that question will put righteousness into action. Loving God begins with your choice to surrender.

2. Surrender is continuous.

The Greek verb "to surrender" indicates a continuous

commitment to the principles of righteousness. It calls us to an ongoing surrender even when it is inconvenient, when it is uncomfortable, and when it is not what we want to do.

3. Surrender is proper.

We are commanded to love the LORD. The name "LORD" reveals that God holds the rightful place of authority over us. He has a divine right to rule in my life. His proper place as Lord would be sufficient in and of itself to require my surrender. He is Master and I am His obedient servant.

4. Surrender is sweet.

Surrender is a positive command that focuses not on duty or activity but rather on my relationship with God. An intimate relationship is always more rewarding than a duty or activity. Good relationships provide the energy for good behavior in the relationship. When we think of who we are surrendering to, it becomes a sweet surrender. "Love the Lord *your* God." This phrase means that we belong to Him in a covenant relationship. We have been adopted by Him according to Ephesians 1:5. Adoption is more significant than birth because adoption is by choice. In the same way, God chose us. He walked into the territory of my life, saw me rebellious in my sin, and by choice He adopted me, and included me in the inheritance of the riches of His glory. He selected me to be a child of the King.

5. Surrender is personal.

We are told to surrender with our heart, soul and mind. No one can impose this surrender on you. It is a personal privilege and responsibility. Refusing to surrender is not rebellion against a parent, pastor or friend; it is rebellion against God and God alone. God is not interested in an empty external relationship. He desires a personal relationship with His children.

6. Surrender is complete.

The word "all" consumes the entirety of what we are. "Love the Lord your God with *all* . . ." We live in a world that negotiates on the basis of percentages. But with Christ, it is nothing short of 100% surrender—heart, soul, mind, strength. He never negotiates on the basis of percentages; every corner of our lives is to be surrendered. There is to be nothing between our soul and our Savior. A limited love is not love at all. A divided loyalty is not love at all. "Seek ye *first* the kingdom of God and His righteousness and all these things shall be added unto you" (Matthew 6:33). For our surrender to be complete, we must love the Lord with *all* our heart, *all* our soul, *all* our mind, and with *all* our strength."

Jonah's Lack of Love for God

There was a serious problem with Jonah's love of God that surfaces in the opening lines of the biblical record. He refused to yield to the will of God for his life. He made a foolish choice to ignore the guidance of God to be used as a voice of light and truth to the Ninevite people. Consequently, one poor choice led to countless others giving evidence that Jonah's love of God at this point was compromised and deficient. Only when we yield continuously to follow obediently the righteous counsel of God is our love of our Savior proven. Jonah's actions revealed that He misunderstood the Lordship of God over his life. Our love of God is proven when we live our lives in humble submission to the authority of God over us. There was no "sweet surrender" in Jonah's story, but rather a contest of wills and a great struggle of the heart. Jonah was blind to the fact that his rebellion was against God and God alone. His love of God was incomplete—divided—and would soon lead to devastating consequences.

It is only by the indwelling of Christ in His divine humility and willing surrender to His Father that we can become truly humble, fully surrendered, and be a witness of what it looks like to truly love God.

Like Jonah, we have our pride from the first Adam. We must, therefore, acquire our humility and surrender from Another Adam—the second Adam (Christ). Pride rules the heart with such terrible power because it is our very Adamic nature. Surrender which brings with it the beauty of humility must become ours in the same way; it must become our very self, our very nature. As natural and easy as it has been to live with pride, we must choose humility to become true lovers of the Most High God.

The absence of the love of God is the secret cause of why the power of God cannot do its mighty work in us. It is only as we, like Jesus, truly know and show that we can do nothing of ourselves, that God can and will do all. It is a sobering thought that our love of God is measured by our everyday relationships and interactions with men and the genuine love it displays. *Our love of God will be found to be a delusion, except as its truth is proven in standing the test of daily life with humanity.*[4] Jonah proved to be sorely lacking in this area of Christian character.

PAUSE TO PONDER

Principles for Godly Living
Loving God Through Surrender

1. Storms wake us up to truths we would otherwise never see.
2. When we walk away from the Most High God, the journey is always down.
3. Defying the revealed will of God goes hand in hand with deception and a deadly destination.
4. When we sin, we always take others with us.
5. When we disobey, we are at great risk both to ourselves and to others who depend upon us.
6. Lifestyle must match theology or the message is at best compromised and at worst negated.
7. We are of no use to God when pride and prejudice remain in the heart.

8. Our love of God is proven when we live our lives in humble submission to God's authority over us.

9. Disobedience and rebellion are proof that our love of God is compromised and lacking.

Questions for Life Application

1. Share a time when you ran away from God because of pride, prejudice or fear. What extreme measures did God use to get you back on track?

2. Like disobedience, obedience also has a price. As people who belong to God's kingdom, we can better understand why Jesus, our Savior and example, would allow Himself to be taken, tortured and crucified to pay for our sins. Share your thoughts about the price of obedience. How does your obedience reveal your love of God?

3. Humility (surrender) is not so much a virtue as it is the root of all the virtues because it alone takes the right attitude before God, allowing Him as God to do all. How does having the root of pride (instead of humility) change your attitude before God?

NOTES

1. Keller, Timothy. *The Prodigal Prophet: Jonah and the Mystery of God's Mercy*. New York, Viking, 2018.

2. Thoughts taken from Stowell, Joseph M. *Fan the Flame*. Chicago, Moody Press, 1986.

3. Stowell. *Fan the Flame*.

4. Murray, Andrew. *Humility: Read and Reflect with the Classics*. Nashville, B&H Publishing Group, 2016.

Story One: A Recap

In selfish pride, Jonah made a tragic choice to nurse his hatred of those unlike himself, thereby withholding God's hope from those he considered undeserving. He ignored God's wisdom for he believed he knew better! It was essential that he become aware of his blindness. The will of God was for Jonah's attitude to change regarding people unlike himself. He was imprisoned in arrogance but simply couldn't see it! We are of no use to God when pride and prejudice remain in the heart. The will of God for Jonah was that his heart begin to beat in perfect rhythm with God's heart, and that of course required a radical change.

This entire ordeal was about exposing ugly heart issues still present within Jonah's soul. He simply refused to love the people he was called to love and serve. He loved hating the Assyrian people, and he rather enjoyed his prideful perspective toward them. After all, their despicable way of life validated his superiority! They were violent, vile, cruel and godless, and he refused to pour out any love upon them. He refused God's orders to go to them—which always means a shipwreck, and unfortunately, the shipwreck always affects others. When we sin, we always take others with us! We carry our influence for good or evil wherever we go!

The consequences of Jonah's disobedience produced repercussions far beyond anything he could have imagined in his worst nightmares!! Tossed overboard into the churning waters, he found himself in a far more frightening place than the sea itself. He came to rest in a surreal, dark, terrifying place—a warm, echoing place—isolated from everyone and everything pleasant, comfortable and familiar. Could this be Sheol—the place of the dead? How could that even be possible? He was aware—awake—alive!

As incomprehensible as it was, he was still living—but living inside a strange, wet murky space—the belly of a gigantic fish! What in heaven's name could God's purpose be in preserving the prophet's life only for him to eventually die in such a hellish fashion?

God always has His reasons for the things that take place in our lives—down to the tiniest details. Thus, it was in this darkness, solitude and uncertainty of a fish's belly that Jonah was finally desperate enough —and humble enough—to turn to his God in utmost submission. In the "prison" of a giant fish, Jonah's entire attitude about everything changed! Life and death, himself and His God, his wisdom and God's wisdom, and particularly the strange assignment that God seemed so determined that he fulfill. The contrast of all these things sharpened for Jonah, bringing fresh insight and perspective. And with a greater desperation than he knew possible, his spirit began to "run" toward the Most High God. Although survival seemed impossible, there was finally the need to reconnect with his God. The pivotal moment came when Jonah lifted up his heart in prayer, and remarkably, in mercy, God heard the humble prayer of his reluctant prophet—and mercy of all mercies the Most High God answered!

> "It is because of the Lord's loving-kindness that we are not consumed. Because His tender compassions never fail. They are new every morning; Great and beyond measure is your faithfulness." (Lamentations 3:22–23)

Story 2

Running To God

Jonah 2

Principle Truth:

The God who allows the waters of life to churn with great frenzy
is the same God who calms them.

Key Concepts:

Doctrine: Hell
Attribute of God: Grace
Character Trait: Loving God through Suffering

Chapter 4

Jonah's Despair and Desperation

The God who allows the waters of life to churn with great frenzy is the same God who calms them.

After being tossed out of the boat by the sailors and into the violent waters, the unfolding of subsequent events took place with record speed. Any attempt to recollect what had brought Jonah to his present state was one enormous blur. Somehow, he now found himself in a deep cavern of sorts—eerily quiet from the anger of the storm, but in motion nonetheless—gliding, it would seem, up and down, at a great pace. Jonah recalled feeling intense panic upon his arrival in this "otherworldly" place. Where in heaven's name was he and how did he get here?

He struggled to reconstruct what he could remember. In his mind, he could still see the face of the frantic captain abruptly waking him to the violent storm certain to take their lives. He recalled as well the unanimous consensus among the sailors that he was the problem and the cause of this tempest. He remembered being tossed over the side of the boat and into the angry sea at his own request. He thought back now about the futility of attempting to swim and survive in waters of a storm so fierce. The look of paralyzing fear on the faces of everyone involved in this frightening scene still haunted him. And then Jonah recalled hitting the turbulent waters and the dreadful terror that seized him as he struggled to breathe. Drowning was a certainty as he realized the impossibility of fighting the elements and more concerning, as his strength grew increasingly weaker from the powerful forces of nature. What more could he do but give in to his exhaustion and the helplessness that enveloped him? The thought of simply surrendering to it all brought a peace his weary soul yearned for.

Then, out of nowhere, some creature of monstrous proportion scooped Jonah up into the air and out of the angry sea. Just when it seemed there was no hope to escape the waters, the unthinkable happened. If his memory served him correctly, it was a gigantic fish that actually swallowed him, and as incredible as this "rescue" seemed, he now found himself in a deep hollow cavity inside the body of this great creature—yes, indeed, in the very belly of this fish; now, no doubt, his "home," his "prison," his certain death!

The air was stale with a strange odor, but obviously adequate enough to keep Jonah alive; air was needed to keep the animal afloat. The heat inside the stomach cavity, however, was quite another matter. It was nearly unbearable, and in no time, contact with the animal's gastric juices attempting digestion of this alien human meal began to affect Jonah's skin producing a painful burning sensation. Unbeknownst to him at the time, the creature's gastric juices were responsible for bleaching his skin and hair snow white! Needless to say, living conditions inside the sea creature were at best miserable as the pressure on his lungs, the panic of his surroundings, and the pain and pressure in his head became increasingly difficult to bear.

As if these bizarre realities were not enough, there was a growing sensation to push upward accompanied by an intense will to live he had never before experienced. Reduced to a pitiful state of desperation, Jonah could only think back of how he had arrived at such a place! Yes, the circumstances were one huge blur, but the horror of this place was anything but a blur! It was all too real and terrifying! How could it be that in just a moment, life can change so abruptly?

It is a mystery, but we live day by day, and we choose in the present in order to shape what is for us an unknown, undetermined future. Only looking back are we able to see the consequences of our actions, and realize their part in the unfolding of our personal story. It is then, with hindsight, that we begin to see how the providence of God guided our steps, leading us precisely to where God intends us to be. Surely our lives are a mysterious combination of our own human action and divine intervention, and most surely the two are inextricably intertwined. As the ancient rabbis often said, "All is foreseen, yet freedom of choice is given!" No doubt the choices Jonah made in running from God met head-on with the providence of the Most High God. God's divine purposes both for Jonah and for Nineveh were indeed unfolding with impeccable precision and perfect timing.

Yes, piecing it all together, Jonah recalled being tossed into the sea, struggling violently to survive the enormous waves, choking almost to death, nearly drowning, seaweed enveloping his head like a noose, the ghastly death struggle at the bottom of the sea, and then, terror of all terrors, the convulsive swallowing action of a gigantic sea creature upon his ever-weakening human body! But by far the greatest horror of all, Jonah was still very much alive! Alive, awake, aware, and more afraid than he could ever remember!

Although helpless, hopeless and utterly desperate, Jonah was indeed alive and greatly humbled to be so! How could it possibly be that he had survived such catastrophic circumstances? It was humanly impossible. Obviously there were powerful spiritual forces at work in these events. Of that fact, Jonah was certain!

As the creature glided across the ocean waters and over the turbulent waves, Jonah realized he was imprisoned in this living hell. Inside the fish, he knew—to his horror—that he was experiencing a form of hell itself, but remarkably what God brought into his mind in that moment of sheer terror were images from familiar Psalms he knew so well that described this place—passages that spoke graphically of just what it was he was now experiencing. How ironic! God was giving Jonah a first-hand experience of a similar place—a very real place to which the godless Ninevites were headed if someone didn't intervene—a place of great darkness, agony, and isolation—a place of eternal separation from the Most High God. The horror of his surroundings put an entirely new perspective on things for this reluctant missionary. Could it be that *this* was God's intention all along? To show Jonah in living color the reality of the place the Bible calls "hell?"

Hell is the eternal destiny of millions of people we encounter every day, unless there is some intervention by the people of God who know the truth and are willing to share it. This striking experience of the reality of such a place—an *eternal* place, a place from which there is no escape—was beginning to work profoundly on Jonah's heart, producing an unfamiliar sense of humility and surrender to the Most High God. He was beginning to realize the truth that indeed there is a fathomless pit of eternal darkness and torment, and even more urgent, there is the desperate need for all to accept God's gracious alternative: His provision and gift of grace through the offer of salvation. Without Christ, there is no hope, and people everywhere must have the opportunity to accept or reject this truth. Certainly this was the case for the Ninevites living in great darkness—in circumstances all too similar to Jonah's present state!

> "Let my prayer come before You and enter into Your presence. Incline Your ear to my cry! For my soul is full of troubles, and my life draws near the grave (Sheol, the place of the dead). I am counted among those who go down to the pit (grave); I am like a man who has no strength (a mere shadow), cast away from the living and abandoned among the dead. Like the slain who live in a nameless grave, whom You no longer remember, and they are cut off from Your hand. You have laid me in the lowest pit, in dark places, in the depths. Your wrath has rested heavily upon me. And You have afflicted me with all your waves. ...But I have cried out to You, O Lord, for help; and in the morning my prayer will come to You." (Psalm 88:2–7,13)

The Hebrew term "fish" is not used in a modern, biological sense. Rather, it refers to a large marine creature—and there are certainly known monsters of the deep large enough to swallow a man whole. In her booklet, *The Bible Today*, Grace Kellogg identifies at least two of them: the sulfur bottom or blue whale and the whale shark; neither of these creatures has any teeth. They feed by opening their enormous mouths, dropping their lower jaws, and moving through the water at high speed, straining food as they go.[1]

A 100-foot sulfur-bottom whale was recorded off Cape Cod in the 1930s. Its mouth was 10 to 12 feet wide—so big it could easily have swallowed a horse. These whales have four to six compartments in their stomachs, any one of which could house a group of full-grown men. The nasal cavity of this whale contains an enormous air storage chamber as well, often measuring seven feet high, seven feet wide, and 14 feet long. If this creature had an unwelcome guest on board that caused a headache, the whale would swim to the nearest land to discharge the offender, just as the great fish did with Jonah.

Interesting as these facts are, we do not need marine biology to prove that a sovereign God can direct the elements of his creation to accomplish His purposes. If we do not believe that God could and did prepare a giant fish to discipline a prophet, then we will have trouble believing that a dead man named Jesus of Nazareth came back to life. Do not forget: it is the three days of Jonah in the belly of a great fish that Jesus used to predict his own resurrection after three days in the grave (Matthew 12:39-40; 16:4; 1 Corinthians 15:4).

GOING DEEPER

THE DOCTRINE OF HELL

"And I saw the beast (the Antichrist) and the kings of the earth, with their armies, gathered together to make war against Him who sits upon the horse and against His army. And the beast (the Antichrist) was captured, and with him the false prophet (the counterfeit Spirit) who in his presence had worked the signs by which he deceived those who had received the mark of the beast, and those who worshipped his image. These two were thrown alive into the *lake of fire that burns with brimstone.*" (Revelation 19:19–20)

Donald Gray Barnhouse in his fine book, *The Invisible War*, states:

"This is the record of the first beings to reach the *eternal lake of fire*, but scripture discloses tragically that it will be filled up with countless lost souls as well when the Son of God moves in for the final judgment. The Bible often uses symbolical language, but it never does so unless there is a thought to be conveyed that is beyond the reach of our present comprehension. The lake of fire, therefore, is either a literal burning lake of fire or something so much worse that there is no human language that approaches the reality. I am convinced that the latter is the correct meaning. In his book *The Great Divorce*, C. S. Lewis describes hell as a dingy town on a dismal day, with sad citizens wandering around in the murky mist performing their aimless and fruitless errands, with no smile seen and no kind word heard. Such a description may well be a valid one for the *outer darkness* of eternal fire. And since God tells us that "every knee shall bow," I would suspect that each individual wears clothing torn at the knees, revealing deep scars and unhealable wounds, silent reminders that before they entered this awful place, some mighty angel seized them bodily and forced them to their knees in the presence of the Lord Jesus Christ before whose glorious Being they were never before willing to bow in humble surrender."[2]

A Definition

Hell: the place of future punishment for the lost, unrepentant, wicked dead. Hell is the final destiny of unbelievers and is described by various images of a furnace of fire, eternal fire, eternal punishment (Matthew 13:42, 50; 25:41, 46), outer darkness, the place of weeping and torment (8:12), the lake of fire, the second death (Revelation 21:8), a place for the devil and his demons (Matthew 25:41). Evidently those in hell experience conscious and everlasting separation from the Lord, never to see the glory of His power (2 Thessalonians 1:9). Those who worshiped the beast mentioned in Revelation will be subject to continuous torment (Revelation 14:1–11).

Other expressions that indicate that the final state of the wicked is eternal are these: "burn with unquenchable fire" (Matthew 3:12), "unquenchable fire where the worm does not die and the fire is not quenched" (Mark 9: 43, 48), there is sin that "will not be forgiven, either in this age or in the age to come" (Matthew 12:32). When Scripture is understood properly, there is no hint anywhere of the termination of the terrible state of unbelievers in hell. Their doom is never ending; there is a solemn finality about their miserable condition. It is significant that the most descriptive and conclusive utterances about hell came directly from the lips of Jesus. A summary of all Scripture that speaks of hell indicates that there is the loss and absence of all that is good, and the misery and torment of an evil conscience. The most terrifying aspect is the complete and deserved separation from a holy God and from all that is pure, holy, and beautiful. There is, as well, the awareness of being under the wrath of God, and of enduring the curse of a righteous and just sentence because of one's sins that were consciously and voluntarily committed.

Nothing can be worse than separation from God and the eternal torment of an evil conscience. Hell is hell for those who are there essentially because they are completely alienated from God, and wherever there is alienation from God, there is always estrangement and isolation from others. This is the worst possible punishment to which anyone could be subject; to be totally and irrevocably cut off from God and to be at enmity with all others. Another painful consequence of such a condition is to be at odds with oneself—literally torn apart from within by an accusing sense of guilt and shame. This condition is one of total conflict; conflict with God, with one's neighbors, and with oneself. This is hell! If the descriptions of hell are figurative or symbolic, the conditions they represent are far more intense and real than the figures of speech by which they are expressed.

Punishment for sin is a persistent teaching of the Bible. The doctrine of the judgment of God is as extensive as the Bible itself. We dare not ignore these imperative teachings. Such passages for reference include:

- Genesis 2:17; 3:17–19; 4:13
- Leviticus 26:27–33
- Psalm 149:7
- Isaiah 2:11
- Ezekiel 14:10
- Amos 1:2–15
- Zechariah 14:19
- Matthew 25:41,46
- Luke 16:23–24
- Romans 2:5–12
- Galatians 6:7–8
- Hebrews 10:29–31
- Revelation 20:11–15

Biblical Terms Used for the Underworld (Place of the Dead)

1. Sheol

The Hebrew word used in the Old Testament for "the grave, the pit, the place of the departed dead." Although *there is not a clear distinction* in the *Old Testament* between the final destiny of the righteous and the wicked, it is evident from various scriptures when studied together, that all alike go to "the grave"—"to the world below," a world of gloom, weariness, darkness, decay and forgetfulness, where one is remote from God, yet accessible to Him. It is a place characterized by silence and rest. Other Old Testament texts, however, suggest some aspect of consciousness, hope and communication in Sheol. A few Old Testament texts suggest the threat of divine judgment after death. On the whole, the very real place known as Sheol was regarded with dismay and foreboding.

At the beginning of *New Testament* times, *there were clear distinctions* between the final destinies of the righteous and the unrighteous as Jesus makes clear in His Parable of the Rich Man and Lazarus from Luke 16. The idea of separate divisions within Sheol for the righteous dead and the unrepentant wicked are clear and unquestionable. It is unmistakable that there was, in Jewish thought, a belief in a future and continued existence beyond death, however shadowy and indefinite the concept.

2. Hades

The Greek word "Hades" in the New Testament is used similarly to "Sheol' in the Old Testament. This word, Hades, was used interchangeably by the translators of the Septuagint (the Greek version of the Old Testament) for Sheol. It designated in general the place or state of the dead, the grave, or death itself. Luke 16 describes Hades as a place of evil and punishment of the wicked and may appropriately be translated "hell" (Luke 16:23). Hades indicates, therefore, nothing more than the place of the dead.

3. Gehenna

The Greek word used in a number of New Testament texts to designate the fiery place of punishment for sinners and is often translated "hell" or "the fires of hell" (Matthew 5:22,29–30; 10:28; 18:9; 23:15,33; Mark 9:43,45,47; James 3:6). It is usually used in connection with the final judgment and suggests that the punishment spoken of is eternal. Gehenna is derived from the Hebrew phrase "valley of Hinnom"—a ravine on the south side of Jerusalem. This unique valley was the center of idolatrous worship in which children were burned by fire as an offering to the heathen god, Molech (2 Chronicles 28:3; 33:6). In the time of young King Josiah, it became a place of abomination, polluted by dead mens' bones and rubbish and by the garbage and filth of Jerusalem that was constantly dumped and burned there. A fire burned continuously in this valley. It thus became a symbol of the "unending fires of hell" where the lost are consumed in torment. It was a symbol of judgment to be imposed on the idolatrous and disobedient. Hades almost always denotes the grave or the place of the dead. Gehenna, a much rarer expression in the new Testament, denotes the eternal fires. Thus, hell as most people think of it, is really Gehenna, not Hades.

4. Tartarus

Another Greek word used to designate hell or "the lower regions" is Tartarus—a classical word for the place of eternal punishment. In Homer's Illiad, Tartarus is described as situated as far below Hades as heaven is above the earth. It was known in ancient Greece as the "prison of the damned." The apostle Peter used this word for the place into which the fallen angels were thrown. ". . . into hell they were committed. To pits of nether gloom (Tartarus) to be kept until the judgment" (2 Peter 2:4).

The Justice of Eternal Punishment

It is difficult for human beings to understand the righteous judgment of a holy God who, on the one hand, hates all evil, yet on the other hand, loves the evildoers enough to sacrifice His only son for their salvation from sin. Divine wrath is the necessary reaction of a holy God who hates all that is contrary to His righteous nature. When the only remedy for human sin is rejected and all appeals of a loving, seeking God for the reconciliation of rebellious sinners are refused, there is no other course of action that God himself can pursue but to leave the sinner to his self-chosen destiny. Punishment for sin is, therefore, the inevitable and inescapable response of divine holiness to that which is morally opposite, and it must continue as long as the sinful condition requiring it continues.

There is no indication anywhere that lost sinners in hell are capable of repentance and faith. If, in this life, they did not turn away from sin and receive Christ as Savior with all the favorable circumstances and opportunities afforded them on earth, it is unreasonable to think they will do so in the life to come. Punishment cannot come to an end until guilt and sin come to an end. When the sinner ultimately resists and rejects the work of the Holy Spirit whereby he is convicted of sin, there remains no more possibility of repentance or salvation. He has committed an eternal sin which deserves eternal punishment. God responds to endless sinning with the necessary counterpart of endless punishment.

God does not choose this destination for people; they freely choose it for themselves. God simply allows them the freedom to choose to reject His truth and subsequently to suffer the full consequences of their evil choice. It must be remembered that God is not only loving, but also holy and righteous. There must be some adequate reckoning with justice in the universe where a revolt against the Most High God has resulted in evil consequences of enormous proportions.

> God responds to endless sinning with the necessary counterpart of endless punishment.

The Bible teaches that although the duration of punishment in hell is eternal for all who have chosen that destiny for themselves, there are degrees of punishment proportional to the degrees of guilt of each individual. Only God is able to determine what those degrees are, and He will assign the consequences with perfect justice according to the responsibilities of each one (Matthew 11:2–24; Luke 12:47–48; Revelation 20:12–13). An obvious comparison is made in these texts between the differing intensities of punishment that are involved in the contrasting privileges, knowledge and opportunities.

Popular Non-biblical Views of the Doctrine of Hell

There are a variety of non-biblical views prevalent today which must be ruled out, however attractively they may be packaged by their advocates and however popular they may become from time to time. Because the biblical doctrine of hell is so offensive to so many, Satan offers the world attractive alternatives—all of which are false and dangerous. The believer must be astute and discerning of any teaching contrary to the inerrant and infallible word of the Most High God (Galatians 1:6–9). The following views are considered erroneous when viewed through the lenses of biblical truth:

1. Universalism—promotes the concept that God will save everyone in the end.
2. Annihilationism—teaches that hell is not a place of conscious suffering but of final extermination.
3. Second Probation—the notion that people can be delivered out of hell. (Purgatory)

The Bible must be our rule of faith for the doctrine of hell, however difficult the doctrine may seem for natural reasons or for human sentiment. Scripture leaves no doubt about the terrible nature and the eternal duration of hell. Rejection or neglect of this doctrine will have dire effects upon the mission of the church.

Jesus Christ's Teaching on Hell

In Luke 16, Jesus told an unusual parable from all the others He taught. The story concerns a rich man who remains unnamed and a poor beggar named Lazarus. It is significant that the rich man is not specifically named and that everything mentioned of him is external. All we are told is the way he dressed and the way he ate. His life was a picture of ultimate extravagance, emptiness and superficiality as he was concerned only with display and self-indulgence. In stark contrast, Jesus painted a picture of a poor man, Lazarus, whose name means "The Lord is my helper," suggesting that this man knew God and was a righteous man. Although he was dirt poor and a beggar, God was his helper.

Lazarus' normal routine was to lay at the gate of the rich man's house daily. He was sick and hungry, his body covered with open sores, but he waited for any scraps of food that might come his way from the rich man's daily feasts. He was never once acknowledged by the rich man whose routine forced him to pass by Lazarus each day. Something profound, however, took place in the lives of these two men that dramatically shifted their earthly state and status. *Death!*

One day just like all the others, the angel of death visited both men and in another dimension, the tables were radically turned. On earth, the rich man no doubt had a magnificent funeral, but interestingly, nothing is said of the burial of the poor man. His body was in all probability thrown out on the city dump outside the city wall, as bodies of beggars customarily were. In the next life, however, Lazarus is the one who is comforted, while the rich man ironically is in agony and utter anguish.

In telling this story, Jesus used vivid metaphors—figurative language—of the place that the men were destined to be. The term used for the destination of Lazarus was "Abraham's Bosom" where the righteous dead go upon their death. This phrase indicates that where Abraham, the father of the faithful resides, there the righteous dead reside as well. We are "sons of Abraham" in this respect, and therefore, upon death we go where Abraham is. Hell is not a question of location but of another dimension entirely. We must think more in terms of dimension rather than location when considering the concept of hell.

Other metaphors Jesus used are: the flames, the water, the tongue and the great chasm—each a symbol that carries great meaning and deep realities. The various symbols convey the existence of a consuming, burning experience—probably that of memory or of desire unfulfilled. It seems that Jesus is indicating that the torment is not necessarily physical only but mental and spiritual as well—perhaps that of loneliness, hopelessness or of despair beyond anything we experience here on earth. These are emotions of an unearthly dimension, and there simply are no words to depict them. Only metaphors come close. Therefore, Jesus is telling us of the reality of a dimension the Bible calls "hell" that is an intensely lonely place—a place of utter isolation. In this story, Jesus is clarifying that in hell there is significantly no one in view—no one, that is, but the rich man himself. He is completely alone—sees no one but himself. C.S. Lewis describes hell as ". . . a place where one becomes more and more himself—his selfish, depraved self!"[3]

The metaphor of "water" in the story is a symbol of relief and in this new dimension the rich man's thoughts are focused only on this one thing—*relief!* He thinks only of the insatiable desire to have Lazarus touch the tip of his tongue with a finger dipped in water. The "chasm" is yet another vivid image of the impossibility of change. We often make the mistake of visualizing hell as a place where the lost are in flames somewhere in the depths of the earth, while above in heaven, the redeemed reside in harmony and peace, and there is a great gulf between the two domains. The "chasm" simply indicates the impossibility of a change in either condition. In other words, no one can pass from one dimension to the other. At this point, the state is fixed and there is no possibility of altering the end result.

It is imperative to understand that this is not what God ever intended or willed for human beings. Judgment and the eternal state of the lost is what the Old Testament prophets refer to as "the strange act of God" (Isaiah 28:21). It is necessary only because of human choice, but it was never intended for human beings, and it is a dimension veiled in mystery.

According to Jesus' story, tragically in hell, the rich man felt something close to love—concern for his brothers. Yet the concern only adds to his torment for at this point, he can do nothing about it. No matter how desperately he wants it to happen, the dead do not come back to warn the living. Perhaps the most agonizing torment of the dead is that at this point, it is impossible to warn the living. There is an insatiable desire to warn but no ability to do so. As the text points out, if the living refuse to hear Moses and the prophets, neither will they be convinced even if one should rise from the dead!

How many who saw the miracles of Jesus still believed in Him at the end of His life? How many stayed with Him because of all His mighty works, His healings, His miracles? Very few! Only a handful of people stood around the cross at Jesus' death. Even after witnessing the raising of Jesus' friend Lazarus from the dead (John 11), the religious leaders and scribes took counsel together plotting to put Jesus to death! When Jesus himself returned from the dead, men still doubted and refused to believe. They still doubt today as countless numbers now claim to be atheists—denying the reality not only of Jesus Christ but even of God Himself!

Jesus' parable teaches that the rich man in life worshiped his empty, materialistic activities, and as a result, had no time or desire to hear of Moses and the prophets. His self-centered life of indulgence was a reflection of that refusal, but he was not in hell because he was rich; he was in hell because he refused the truth of God as given through the law and the prophets. Lazarus, on the other hand, was in heaven because he believed Moses and the prophets, and because he believed, he made God his helper and trusted in Him. He was not in heaven merely to be given compensation for what he endured on earth. There will be many a poor man in hell, just as there will be many who are rich in heaven. Lazarus was in Paradise (Abraham's Bosom) simply because he believed Moses and the prophets—the truth of the Most High God.

The point of the parable is this: then (Eternity) is always determined by now. We are placed here now to know and accept what is real—to distinguish between good and evil, and live our lives here in light of our eternal destiny there. Unless we learn these things now, there will be no glorious life to come. We learn to live this way by hearing the truth of God, receiving it and living it out. There is indeed an eternal destination that awaits those who reject the truth of the Most High God. When we understand the horror, agony and eternal state of this place, the urgency to share God's truth must become first and foremost. As Hudson Taylor said, "The Great Commission is not an option to be considered, it is a command to be obeyed."

Jonah's Assignment to Nineveh

Fearing God and walking in obedience to His commandments is the ultimate purpose of the life of every man. The reason for one's earthly existence is that we might learn, through the revelation of the Most High God, the realities of what human life is meant to be and the certain realities that lie beyond this life—what this life is hurtling toward and what its final expression will be, how the decisions, choices and actions here determine the eternal state of our soul there. The spirit and soul of man never die; they live on in one dimension or the other—there is no in-between and no possibility of change after this life. Everything in this life must relate to this reality to have any meaning and purpose at all.

Our God is a missionary God—full of love, mercy, grace, and compassion. He intends that no man live without the knowledge of this truth. It is the mercy of God to impart the revelation of this truth—the truth of hell—to be included in countless scriptures throughout both Old and New Testament teaching. The lost people of Nineveh were on God's heart and in great need of hearing the truth for this was soon to be their reality apart from God's intervention. Therefore, Jonah's assignment was urgent and vitally important simply because he was chosen to be God's messenger of this truth. Although Jonah was disregarding the voice of God and his assignment, and running in the opposite direction, God was moving heaven and earth to give Jonah a second chance at his calling. He is willing that no one perish but that *all* have the opportunity to know and learn of Him. Yes, even the wicked Ninevites!

PAUSE TO PONDER

Principles For Godly Living
Hell

1. Nothing can be worse than separation from God, and the eternal torment of a sinful conscience.

2. Divine wrath is the necessary reaction of a holy and just God who hates all that is contrary to His righteous nature.

3. God does not send people to hell; they freely choose it for themselves.

4. Because the biblical doctrine of hell is offensive to so many, Satan offers the world attractive alternatives, all of which are false and dangerous.

5. The Bible must be our guide for understanding the reality and the nature of hell.

6. "Hell is a place where one becomes more and more himself—his selfish, depraved self." C.S. Lewis

7. Hell was never intended for human beings.

8. We are placed on earth to know and accept what is reality and truth—to distinguish between good and evil, and to live our lives *here* in light of our eternal destiny *there*.

9. The Great Commission is not an option to be considered, it is a command to be obeyed.

10. The spirit and soul of man never die—they live on in one dimension or the other—there is no in between and no possibility of change after this life.

Questions for Life Transformation

How has the study of the doctrine of hell created an urgency in your heart to share the message of God's truth and grace with others? Who in your circle of influence needs your witness? Name them and pray for them now! Are you willing to share the truth with them no matter the cost? How does Jonah's example move you to action?

NOTES

1. Jeremiah, David. "Swallowed by a Great Fish – Jonah 1:17." *David Jeremiah Study Bible*. Franklin, Worthy Publishing, 2016.

2. Barnhouse, Donald G. *The Invisible War*. Grand Rapids, Zondervan, 1995.

3. Lewis, C.S. *The Great Divorce*. New York, Harper Collins Publishers, 1973.

Chapter 5

Jonah's Dedication and Deliverance

The God who allows the waters of life to churn with great frenzy is the same God who calms them.

"We can never find God's amazing grace at the high points of our lives, but in the valleys and depths, at the bottom. No human heart will learn its sinfulness and impotence by being told it is sinful. It will have to be shown — often in brutal experience. No human heart will dare to believe in such free, costly grace unless it is the **only** hope."[1]

The great missionary to China, Hudson Taylor said, "Do not have your concert first, and then tune your instrument afterwards. Begin the day with the word of God and prayer, and get first of all into harmony with Him." Jonah knew God's word, particularly the Psalms. The word of God had been memorized—sung—used in Israelite worship, and therefore, planted deeply within the prophet's heart. Along with all his fellow Israelites, he knew what it was to praise the Most High God through the beauty of the Scriptures, and thus, these were the words that came flooding into his heart and mind in his moment of great despair and desperation.

Knowing the word of God throughout the course of a lifetime is the essential "life preserver" for the most perilous storms of this life.

Only a fool waits until the crisis arrives and expects to be prepared for what faces him. If he hasn't taken the time to add to his knowledge, faith, and to faith, endurance to press on in the great battles of life, he will not be equipped to face the storm. We must use the good times in life to prepare for the inevitable storms that are sure to come, for when the storm comes, there is no time and certainly no focus except for the calamity facing us head on.

Therefore, with an instinctive response, Jonah cried out to God in words all too familiar to him. In his head, he had no doubt that the words of the Psalms were true, but these words were now true for Jonah specifically and for his particularly dire situation. It was as if the words now had new meaning and had been written specifically for him—for his particular experience. It is ironic but oh, so true, that the best place to learn of God's grace is when we are at rock bottom. It was not simply being at the bottom, however, that began to change Jonah's heart—it was prayer at the bottom where Jonah was fully focused on his God, totally dependent upon Him, and isolated from all distraction. Therefore, the way "up" was first of all "down"—both for Jonah's circumstances in the raging waters and regarding his spiritual journey of faith as well. When at the "bottom," we are forced to finally look up! It was essential, therefore, that Jonah be brought to the end of himself, and the Most High God was orchestrating events to insure that outcome.

> Knowing the word of God throughout the course of a lifetime is the essential "life preserver" for the most perilous storms of this life.

Interestingly, as he began to pray, his thoughts settled upon one foundational, rock-solid truth—the grace of God. His prayer came pouring forth from a humble heart as a declaration of God's remarkable grace based out of words that had been spoken centuries earlier through the writer of the Psalms he knew so well. When there were no words of his own for the agony he endured, it was the words of the living God that automatically took over. "Thy word is a lamp unto my feet and a light unto my path" (Psalms 119:105).

Jonah's prayer reflected thoughts penned centuries earlier by an obscure descendant of Korah whose situation, no doubt, perfectly fit Jonah's circumstance. The meditation echoed in Jonah's prayer comes from Psalm 88, written by Heman the Ezrahite (a descendant of Korah whose story is told in the book of Numbers). Of all the psalms in the Bible, 11 are attributed to the sons of Korah, and these psalms comprise some of the most treasured writings of the Psalter. Psalms such as the following are well-loved and some of the most beautiful writing found in all of the holy Scriptures:

> We must use the good times in life to prepare for the inevitable storms that are sure to come, for when the storm comes, there is no time and certainly no focus except for the calamity facing us head on.

> "As the deer pants for flowing streams, so pants my soul for you, O God." Psalm 42:1 (". . . of the sons of Korah")

> Psalm 84:1 states, "How lovely is your dwelling place, O God." (". . . of the sons of Korah")

> Psalm 46:1–3: "God is our refuge and strength, an ever present help in trouble. Therefore, we will not fear, though the earth give way and the mountains fall into the heart of the sea, though its waters roar and foam and the mountains quake with their surging." (". . . a psalm of the sons of Korah")

It is ironic that Korah, the distant ancestor of the writers of these psalms, perished in an earthquake for his pride and rebellion (Numbers 16:28–35). From the psalms of his descendants, our own songs of hope and renewed purpose flow out of hearts of humility as we too recall like Jonah, our own fallen state from which God alone can deliver us.

Deliverance comes only through His grace. This was certainly the case for the sons of Korah. Their gifts of poetry and music resonate with the beauty of God's grace upon sinful humanity. It was no doubt the case with Jonah as well as he recalled the words which framed his own prayer of desperation, and it should be so with believers of the twenty-first century. We must *know* the Scriptures to survive the storms of life, for they become our voice when circumstances render us speechless!

The writer of Psalm 88 is clinging to God as he pours out his pain in his own darkest hour. Like Jonah, he held tightly to a God he no longer understood and whom he feared no longer loved him. From where he stood, it appeared that God had forgotten him, cut him off from His care, driven his friends away, rejected him, and left him with only darkness for company. That is what God looked like to the writer of Psalm 88. However, what makes the prayer of Psalm 88 so remarkable is just that—*it is a prayer*. To be in a spirit of prayer is to hold on to God as tightly as one can—no matter how strong the temptation is to let go. The psalmist (and Jonah) refuse to fall into a cynical silence but instead keep the conversation going even though the "exchange" seems to be maddeningly one sided. Therefore, reminiscent of the desperation of the psalmist, Jonah, from the belly of the fish, prayed to his God in similar fashion:

> We must know the Scriptures to survive the storms of life, for they become our voice when circumstances render us speechless!

"In my distress, I called to You, Lord, and You answered me. From the depths of the grave, I called for help and You listened to my cry. You hurled me into the deep, into the very heart of the seas, and the currents swirled about me; all Your waves and breakers swept over me. I said to myself, I have been banished from your sight. O Lord; yet *I will* look again toward Your holy temple. The engulfing waters threatened me, the deep surrounded me; seaweed was wrapped around my head. To the roots of the mountains I sank down below; the earth beneath barred me in forever. But You, O God, brought my life up from the pit, O Lord, my God. When my life was ebbing away, I remembered You, Lord, and my prayer rose to You, to Your holy temple. Those who cling to worthless idols forfeit the grace that could be theirs. But I, with a song of thanksgiving, will sacrifice to you. What I have vowed, *I will* make good. Salvation and deliverance come only from the Lord." (Jonah 2)

When the living God heard the effectual, fervent prayer of this now greatly humbled servant, He commanded the fish and it vomited Jonah onto dry land! Jonah's petrifying experience became his ultimate purifying experience. By the mercies of God alone, there was still a task to accomplish, and God's intention was to offer Jonah undeserved grace and a second chance to fulfill the assignment. The Ninevites were still living in darkness and God's intention was for them to hear the truth of His love and grace.

The God who allows the waters of life to churn with great frenzy is the same God who calms them. God's divine purpose for Jonah's life was for him to fulfill his calling. Thus, He performed remarkable miracles to insure that Jonah had a second chance to accomplish that purpose. Would all that Jonah had experienced in the deep prove to be enough to redirect this reluctant prophet into submission to God's will? Would his gratitude for a miraculous deliverance be enough to surrender to God to the point of going to Nineveh? Or could it be that the roots of his pride were still so deeply engrained that even these harsh life lessons so recently endured were not enough? Only time would tell.

Believers must pay particular attention to our part in the commission mandate God sets forth. Every believer is called to go. The Great Commission is a "co-mission" which involves the *cooperation of master and servant.* In His last words to His disciples found in Matthew 28, Jesus presented the Great Commission, and moments before His ascension into heaven, He gave instructions that are neither optional nor meant for pastors and missionaries only. The call is for all—all believers must co-operate in this great endeavor of advancing the Kingdom of God on earth! We are called to go and make disciples of all nations. We must, therefore, be willing to leave safety, security, preconceptions, pride, prejudice and anything else that might hinder the advancement of the gospel in order to proclaim this good news of salvation to the lost.

We must never forget that there is a vast difference between this life and the next. It is only God's kingdom, His "city," that has foundations that will last. It is only God's will, His approval, protection and eternal inheritance that are permanent as Jonah was beginning to learn (the hard way). Jonah's prideful choices stemmed from a deadly blindness at work in his heart regarding God's grace towards *all* people. The tragedy was the fact that he simply could not see that he too was in need of the grace of God just as much as were the wicked Ninevites.

It was God's grace upon his own life that had preserved and protected him throughout his disobedience. At the beginning of his journey, Jonah wrestled with this mystery in regard to God's intentions to extend His grace to the godless. He simply could not comprehend the merciful heart of his God. In the belly of the fish, he wrestled once more with this recurring theme of God's grace, and based upon his prayer recorded in chapter two, it is evident that only when he voiced fresh insight into this mysterious attribute (of God's grace) was he released onto dry land. It was as if Jonah's understanding of *grace* as stated in his prayer was indeed *the key* that removed the scales from his eyes, opened up the belly of the fish, and set free God's prophet from his hellish prison!

God's intention in it all was to give Jonah a fresh understanding of grace—God's *amazing, matchless* grace—the most incredible thing that can ever be offered to any person—any sinner lost in rebellion—whether that sinner is like the prodigal son lost in disobedience and defiance or like the elder brother, lost in good works and legalism! We are all sinners in desperate need of grace. There are *no* exceptions! Ignorance in understanding this gift of God causes disastrous problems—all of which end in personal prisons of all sorts. Until we truly understand God's grace and see its profound application for our own personal lives, we like Jonah, are just a shadow of what we can be and should be—and more importantly, what God intends for us to be.

The truth of the matter is that the doctrine of God's grace is that which sets Christianity apart from all other faiths. It is the central message of our salvation, the *good* news—the *gospel.* The Apostle Paul eloquently proclaims the impact of this "grace" upon genuine, born-again believers in his letter to the Colossian church of the first century:

"The *gospel* is bearing fruit and growing throughout the whole world—just as it has been doing among you since the day you heard it and truly understood God's grace" (Colossians 1:6). *Understanding the grace of God, therefore, is the key to church growth and the propagation of the gospel.*

Indeed, it is the understanding and acceptance of God's grace (through faith) that makes a person a Christ follower. We must ask God for fresh understanding of this gift from God in our own personal experience. A moral person, a religious person or a nice person is not necessarily a genuine Christian or Christ follower. It is God's grace that is the foundation of our faith, and that which sets the Christian and the Christian faith apart.

> "For it is by grace (God's remarkable compassion and undeserved favor drawing you to Christ) that you have been saved (actually delivered from judgment and given eternal life) through faith. And this salvation is not of yourselves (not through your own efforts) but it is the undeserved gracious gift of God; not as a result of your works nor your attempts to keep the Law, so that no one will be able to boast or take credit in any way for his salvation." (Ephesians 2:8–9)

According to Martin Luther:

"Faith is a living bold trust in God's grace, so certain of God's favor that it (faith) would risk death a thousand times trusting in it. Such confidence and knowledge of God's grace makes you happy, joyful, and bold in your relationship to God and all creatures. The Holy Spirit makes this happen through faith."[2]

This aspect of Jonah's relationship with God was obviously lacking. Indeed the issue of God's grace was the aspect of gross spiritual deficiency that had to be exposed and addressed before Jonah could be of any use to God! He had no compassion for the Ninevites because he couldn't see the very grace of God operating in his own life—the same grace God commissioned him to extend to them! He took for granted God's grace because he was a "chosen Israelite," but he struggled terribly with the fact that God intended this same grace for the Ninevites as well. God, however, loved Jonah and refused to overlook his sin with a shrug. In fact, He was willing to go to *extreme measures* to insure that Jonah understood His grace and was recommissioned for his assignment.

If we think that just because we are believers in Jesus Christ, we can live any way we choose, then we too are guilty as was Jonah of espousing a form of "cheap grace"—taking sin lightly and failing to realize what an enormous cost it was for God to give us this gift through the death of His only son. When we realize that our salvation cost Jesus His glory in heaven and His physical life on earth, that it entailed unimaginable suffering, then and only then can we begin to see that grace is not cheap but indescribably costly (Philippians 2:1–11). Unless we see what it cost Christ to save us from our sin, we will never understand the delight of obedience and service—even when our obedience may require surrender, suffering and sacrifice. As J.I. Packer states: "Love awakens love in return; and love, once awakened, desires to give pleasure."[3]

Jonah, when delivered from the belly of the fish, did indeed journey to Nineveh. He carried out his mission, *but* he did it with no heart— evidence that his understanding of God's grace was still grossly lacking!

He simply went through the motions of what he perceived obedience to God's command to be, without a heart of love for those he went to serve. We are left to wonder in the end if he ever really "got it" (the mystery of God's grace). The book ends with the question unanswered.

It is tragic to live an entire lifetime and fail to grasp the beauty of God's grace toward us personally. It prevents one from having the kind of personal relationship God intends for every believer. It limits the impact of one who claims to love God with all his heart greatly minimizing the impact for kingdom progress. It leads to a life of impotence and shallowness. It is responsible for the weakness so prevalent in the twenty-first century body of Christ. May God use the story of Jonah to awaken the reader's heart to the infinite, beautiful, matchless grace of God.

GOING DEEPER

ATTRIBUTE OF GOD: GRACE

A Definition

Grace: The gift of God as expressed in His actions of extending mercy, loving-kindness and salvation to people. Grace is the incomprehensible dimension of divine activity that enables God to confront human indifference and rebellion with an inexhaustible capacity to forgive and to bless. God's grace is manifested through action. The doctrine of salvation through God's grace is the foundational of thought in both the Old and New Testaments. The Old Testament anticipates and prepares for the full expression of grace that becomes truly manifest in the New Testament through the finished work of Jesus Christ.

Grace in the Old Testament

Early in the narrative of the Old Testament, God reveals Himself as a "God, merciful and gracious, slow to anger, and abounding in steadfast love and faithfulness" (Exodus 34:6). As a result, it becomes possible for undeserving human beings to approach Him in a spirit of humility, prayer and supplication: ". . . If now I have found favor (grace) in thy sight, O Lord . . ." (Exodus 34:9). Through God's divine initiative, human separation from God is turned by Him into a state of undeserved acceptance; thus, opening the way for reconciliation and redemptive usefulness along with kingdom impact as well.

Divine grace was already operative in the Garden of Eden when God responded to the devastating effects of the fall with His promise of redemption (Genesis 3:15) and loving care rather than with abandonment or annihilation. God's call to Abraham was an extension of His grace as well, not only solely to the patriarch but through him—as a means of universal outreach to his descendants and to all people. God's grace, through Abraham, would become the means of blessing "all the families of the earth" (Genesis 12:2–3). Consequently, both the election of Abraham and God's promise of worldwide blessing to all nations find their expression in a God-given covenant of grace. Therefore, the election of Abraham and of national Israel was never intended to be an end in itself. It was, rather, God's plan for extending His redemptive purposes to all believers from every nation, tribe and tongue. In extending His grace to Abraham, God established the channel of redemptive opportunity for all believers from all nations as well as the very beginnings of His church universal—God's community of *grace* operating powerfully through a body of believers.

Grace in the New Testament

According to Hebrews 8, the institutions of the Old Covenant (Mosaic laws and sacrificial system) possessed only a temporary validity that has been superseded by the ultimate manifestations of God's grace in the New Covenant (Hebrews 8:6–7). Consequently the Old Covenant was to become obsolete and replaced by a New Covenant that would display the full and completed manifestation of the grace of God (Jeremiah 31:33; Matthew 26:28; 2 Corinthians 3: 9–11; Hebrews 8:13; Hebrews 9:15).

The Grace of God Revealed in the Person of Christ

The concept of divine grace regarding God's active involvement in human affairs receives a much sharper focus in the New Testament. God's grace became fully manifested in the very person of Jesus Christ who demonstrated visibly the dynamic nature of God's undeserved favor, and fulfills in His earthly ministry the Old Covenant promises that pertain to God's gracious dealings with humanity. God's grace manifested in Jesus Christ makes it possible for God to forgive sinners and to gather them as a body of believers called the church, the new covenant community.

During His earthly ministry, Jesus repeatedly pronounced words of forgiveness and grace upon a great number of sinners, and ministered God's undeserved favor upon a host of desperate human needs as well. Jesus made it clear that His purpose for coming was to seek and save the lost, but ultimately, it was His redemptive death on the cross that opened wide the gate of salvation for repentant sinners to find *direct access* to His forgiveness and grace.

Luke 23:45 and Mark 15:38 both testify of the dramatic access into the very presence of God made possible through the death of Jesus as the veil of the Jewish temple was torn into from top to bottom. This simple but profound truth is articulated by the apostle Paul in his explanation of the doctrine of justification by faith through *grace* (Romans 3:23; Titus. 3:7). According to the teachings of Paul, God's gracious provision of the substitutionary death of His son, Christ Jesus, enabled Him to pronounce a verdict of "justified" or "not guilty" on repentant sinners and to remarkably include them in His eternal purposes. As a result, they enter into the realm of God's gracious activity, enabling them to enter into the life-long process of individual sanctification in cooperation with the Holy Spirit. (Sanctification: the lifelong process of becoming more and more like Jesus.)

The Benefits of God's Grace to His Children

God's grace provides undeserved benefits and gifts that enrich our lives and unite us together as "the church," the body of Christ. Our divine acceptance on the basis of God's grace gives us a brand new status as children of God, members of the household of God, so that we relate to God as a personal Heavenly Father (Galatians 4:4–6). Consequently, we become members of a community where race, class and sexual distinctions are irrelevant since we all become equal inheritors of God's age-long promise to Abraham of universal blessing.

The Holy Spirit graciously energizes believers with a variety of spiritual gifts—given by God—for the performance of various ministries designed to benefit the entire body of believers—the church. Because the riches of God's grace are freely lavished upon believers in their community life upon earth, the church demonstrates by its very existence, the immeasurable riches of God's grace available through a relationship with Jesus Christ.

Humility and the Grace of God

As a result of the grace given to us as God's children, we are to likewise reflect this grace in our own Christian character and relationships. The indisputable condition for receiving God's grace is a humble spirit and surrender to the authority of Almighty God, and such humility in relation to God enables the believer to likewise practice humility in regard to others. Because of God's grace extended mercifully to the believer, the believer can thus set aside selfishness, superiority, pettiness and conceit in order to treat others with compassion and grace in an attitude of mutual servanthood, respect and forgiveness. Because we have been forgiven, we too must forgive (not an option!), and extend grace and mercy to others. As children of the God of grace, we are commanded to grow in this same grace of the Lord (2 Peter 3:18).

Remarkably, the Bible declares God's grace to be fully accessible to all humans with no other precondition except that of a repentant desire to receive it. As a result the human condition of alienation from God and His purposes is replaced with access and freedom to approach the otherwise unapproachable majesty of a holy and righteous God. It is God's grace freely extended to sinners that cancels and annihilates any tendency for boasting. Freely we receive it—freely we are to give it.

Jonah and the Grace of God

Not until Jonah was stripped of his own self-sufficiency was deliverance possible. There was a fatal flaw in Jonah's character and it had lain dormant as long as his life was going well. It was through complete failure that he began to see it and change it. Countless Christians attest to the same experience. So often, it is only when one reaches the "bottom," when everything falls apart, when all of one's schemes and resources are broken and exhausted, that one is finally open to complete dependence upon the grace of God alone. How true is the saying: you never realize that Jesus is all you need until Jesus is all you have. You must lose your life to find your life, and so often the best place to learn the deepest secrets of God's grace is at the "bottom."

As Jonah prayed in the belly of the fish, his mind "took captive" this foundational concept of God's grace—a picture in itself of the covenant love and mercy of God. It took the entire prayer for Jonah to get to his final declaration, but once he acknowledged and claimed God's grace, interestingly he was released back into the land of the living with renewed purpose and a grateful heart. For once in his life, the grace of God upon him was unmistakable!

For many, the grace of God is just an abstract word, a concept with little life-changing power. This is the case because certain key truths about God's grace have never been processed and felt deeply in the human heart. In the depths of despair and through fervent prayer to the God of all grace, Jonah came to understand three life-changing truths.

1. We are All Guilty Sinners in Need of the Grace of God.

The first critical truth we must acknowledge, process and accept is that the Bible's persistent message is true. We *are* indeed guilty sinners—all of us—in desperate need of the grace of God. Jonah states this in his prayer: "*You* cast me into the deep, into the heart of the seas" (2:3). He boldly acknowledges and knows in the deepest recesses of his soul that there is divine justice, and that *he deserved what he was experiencing.*

2. We Cannot Fix Ourselves

We must come to the place where we admit not only our sins but also that we cannot repair or cleanse ourselves from them. The present twenty-first century culture does not help us here for it is dominated by therapy, technology and instant "fixes." Even if we accept responsibility for wrongdoing, we are tempted always to believe "we can fix this." We believe that with hard work or religious observance, we can repair what is broken. But this is folly! We cannot fix what is wrong with us—only God can. Only His grace upon us can restore us to a right standing with Him.

The false assumption that we can fix ourselves is a foundational premise of every major world religion. But in verse six, Jonah rejects this! He realizes that he is helpless to save himself. He says he is sinking to "the netherworld," the underwater world farthest from living humanity and God who is in His temple, and that there "its bars are closed upon me forever." He realizes that he stands condemned and permanently barred from God because of his sin and rebellion, and there is no possible way to open those gates himself or make good his debt. The grace of God operates only when one acknowledges a desperate sense of need and a recognition of one's inability to help himself. We are barred from God and His grace until we admit that *we cannot save ourselves.*

3. God Grace is Costly

Not once but twice in his prayer, Jonah looks not merely toward heaven but "toward your holy temple" (2:4) and "to the temple of your holiness" (2:7). Why is this significant? It shows that Jonah knew that it was over the mercy seat in the temple that God promised to speak to us. "There I will meet with you; from above the mercy seat, from between the two cherubim which are on the Ark of the Testimony, I will speak" (Exodus 25:22). The mercy seat was a slab of gold over the top of the Ark of the Covenant, in which resided the tablets of the 10 Commandments. On the Day of Atonement, a priest sprinkled the blood of the atoning sacrifice for the sins of the people on the mercy seat. The temple was the residence of the holy God, His perfect moral righteousness represented by the 10 Commandments, which no human being has or ever can keep.

How then shall we approach God? The law of God condemns us. Yes indeed it does—*except for the blood* of the atoning sacrifice on the mercy seat, over the 10 Commandments, shielding us from its condemnation. It is only when the death of a substitute secures our forgiveness that we can speak and commune with God. A better picture of the gospel of Jesus Christ and what He accomplished on our behalf on the cross can hardly be imagined! The temple and the Old Testament sacrificial system established all three of these critical truths as its very foundation. *We are sinners, unable to save ourselves and able to be saved only through the extreme and costly death of a perfect Substitute.* Not until centuries later would it be revealed that atonement could not be accomplished by the blood of bulls and goats but *only by the once-for-all sacrifice of Jesus Christ* (Hebrews 10:4–10).

Only when we fully believe, grasp and remind ourselves of these three foundational and life-transforming truths can we appropriate, process and fully grasp the incredible, undeserving grace and unmerited favor of God upon our lives. We must acknowledge and accept that as sinners, we deserve nothing but condemnation, that we are utterly incapable of saving ourselves, and that God in great mercy has saved us by His grace despite our sin, at infinite cost to Himself. Only then will we be able to sing, as the hymn writer declares:

". . . lost in wonder, love and praise" at the lengths and depths to which God in Christ has gone in bestowing this amazing grace upon us.[4]

Because Jesus Christ represents the fulfillment, the embodiment, and the dispenser of divine grace, the early Christians freely referred to God's grace as "the grace of our Lord Jesus Christ." This grace was conceived as being so basic and so pervasive to their individual lives and to the existence of their communities of faith that they naturally coupled the traditional greeting of "Shalom" (Peace) with a reference to the "Grace of Jesus Christ." This is the reason for the repetition of numerous variations on the basic greeting formula found in almost every book of the New Testament: "The grace of our Lord Jesus Christ be with you all" (2 Thessalonians 3:18).

PAUSE TO PONDER

Principles for Godly Living
God's Grace

1. Knowing the word of God throughout the course of a lifetime is the essential "life preserver" for the most perilous storms of life.
2. Only a fool waits until the crisis arrives and expects to be prepared for what faces him.
3. We must use the good times in life to prepare for the inevitable storms that are sure to come, for when the storm comes, there is no time and certainly no focus except for the calamity facing us head on.
4. When there are no words for the agony we face, it is the words of the living God that must take over.
5. We must know the Scriptures to survive the storms of life, for they become our voice when circumstances render us speechless.
6. Until we truly understand God's grace and see its profound application for us personally, we, like Jonah, are just a shadow of what we can be and should be, and more importantly what God intends for us to be.

7. Understanding the amazing grace of God and appropriating it is the key to church growth and the propagation of the gospel.

8. Because we have been forgiven, we too must forgive and extend grace and mercy to others.

9. God's grace is fully accessible to all humans with no other precondition except that of a repentant heart and the desire to receive it.

10. It is God's grace freely extended to sinners that cancels and annihilates any tendency for boasting.

Questions for Life Transformation

1. How much of God's word have you hidden in your heart in preparation for life's storms? What action do you need to take to better prepare yourself? Will you allow the truth of this story to help you establish a plan of action to memorize portions of the Bible so that you will be ready to face the inevitable storms certain to come? In obedience to God, write out *your* plan—*now*! (Be ready to share it at our next meeting.)

2. How has your understanding of God's grace become more personal to you through the study of Jonah 2? Explain in your own words the principle from John Newton mentioned in the story: "Everything is needful that He sends; Nothing is needful that he withholds." How does your understanding of this principle deepen your trust of God's sovereignty in the difficult things He has allowed in your life?

NOTES

1. Keller, Timothy. *The Prodigal Prophet: Jonah and the Mystery of God's Mercy.* New York, Viking, 2018.

2. Luther, Martin. "Martin Luther's Definition of Faith." *Ligonier Ministries,* https://www.ligonier.org/learn/articles/martin-luthers-definition-of-faith/. Accessed 3 March 2020.

3. Packer, J.I. *Knowing God.* Downers Grove, InterVarsity Press, 1973.

4. Wesley, Charles. "Love Divine, All Loves Excelling." 1947. *Hymnary.org,* https://hymnary.org/text/love_divine_all_love_excelling_joy_of_he. Accessed 2 March 2020.

Chapter 6

Greater Miracles and Lesser Miracles

The God who allows the waters of life to churn with great frenzy is the same God who calms them.

Scripture always strengthens prayer. Jonah's well-trained mind was directed straight to God's word as he prayed the words right back to his Heavenly Father—a powerful formula to an effective prayer life! Knowing God's word is the best insurance policy for those times in life when we find ourselves in desperate straits. Prayer is a two-way conversation. God speaks through the Bible to us, and we speak to God through prayer. God speaks and we listen. Jonah did this in his extremity. He instantly recalled God's voice through the Scriptures that over the years had become deeply embedded in his heart, and he prayed them. This is the way our prayers are so often answered. Therefore, when we pray *God's words*, we can be assured that we are praying His will.

God indeed allows His children to be tested—at times in ways that take us to our limits—but He promises never to test us above or beyond what we are able to bear (1 Corinthians 10:13). He has promised His children a way of escape in the trial that often comes through the power that is ours through this Word. "For the word of God is living and active and full of power. It is sharper than any two-edged sword, penetrating as far as the division of the soul and spirit and of both joints and of marrow exposing and judging the very thoughts and intentions of the heart" (Hebrews 4:12). Often it is the word of God that supplies the believer with "a way of escape." We, like Jonah, must know it! It must be hidden in the heart.

In a very real sense, the word of God that came to Jonah's mind brought forth the very miracle that led to his release! His thoughts connected him to the powerful Spirit of God, thus shifting his thinking from desperation and darkness to humble gratitude and praise for the remarkable and mysterious grace of his God! God's omnipotence was certainly evident through the miracle of Jonah being swallowed by the fish and surviving; however, the *greater miracle* was that Jonah was sustained inside the fish's belly for three days by the power and the providence of the Most High God. Jonah had been given a vitally important task and God's intention was for him to accomplish it. The lesser miracle was that his life was spared. The *greater miracle* was that Jonah's heart was changed. The greatest miracle God can ever perform in an individual is a transformed life. The lesser miracle was that the storm was stilled physically— the *greater miracle* was that the spiritual storm of pride and prejudice inside his heart was finally broken (to some extent!). Jonah's obedience to fulfill his calling was finally back on course. Therefore, with the miracle of a heart now more in line with God's purposes, Jonah was on the way to Nineveh through the miracle of God's grace and a second chance.

> The greatest miracle God can ever perform in an individual is a transformed life.

It is insightful to notice that Jonah's prayer moved from a state of desperation to a plea for deliverance, but ends with a song of praise and thanksgiving! The progression indicates the shift in his thinking; Jonah came to see that life is not about us—it is about God's glory and fulfilling His purposes in His way.

EXAMINING JONAH'S PRAYER /
DISCOVERING GOD'S "WAY OF ESCAPE"

The Desperation

"Out of the belly of Sheol I cry, and *you hear my voice* . . .

"Sheol" was the realm of divine punishment and death. To speak of already being in such a place was an expression of Jonah's extreme anguish and pain. The metaphor conveys a despair of the darkest reality. Jonah knew his suffering was a penalty, and that his sin had banished him from God's sight. He was desperate, hopeless, and sensed abandonment from God.

For You cast me into the deep . . . All your waves and your billows pass over me . . . I am driven away from your sight . . ."

The Plea For Deliverance and The Song of Praise

"When my life was ebbing away, I remembered You, Lord, and my prayer rose to You, to Your holy temple. Those who cling to worthless idols, forfeit the *grace* that could be theirs. But I, with a song of thanksgiving, will sacrifice to You. What I have vowed, I will make good. Salvation and deliverance come from You alone."

When Jesus called himself one "greater than Jonah," He was referring to the three days and nights Jonah spent in the deep (Mathew 12:40–41). And just as Jonah pleaded with God for deliverance, so did Jesus ask for "the cup" of suffering to be taken from Him. On the cross, Jesus' suffering reminds us of the great suffering of Jonah, but to an infinitely greater degree. As Jesus cried out to His Father, "My God, My God, why have you forsaken me?" we think as well of Jonah in the depths of the sea crying out for deliverance to his God.

We must, however, remember the great contrast between the two situations. Jonah was thrown into the sea because of his sinful choice to run from God and in order to save the sailors. Jesus, our Savior, went willingly into the depths of death and separation from God—hell itself, as a sinless substitute—in order to save Jonah and all of mankind from the penalty of sin. Jonah was crushed under the weight of the waves and breakers (Jonah 2:3) of God's waters, but Jesus was buried and crushed under the waves of God's wrath as He took upon himself our sin.

Jonah states that he was in Sheol—the place of the dead—driven from God's sight. The Apostles' Creed spoken regularly in millions of churches across the world today states that—for our sake, Jesus "descended into hell." The truth of the Bible declares that Jesus suffered physically in the plain sight of men but also took the invisible and incomprehensible judgment (the wrath of a holy God which He underwent in the sight of God) in order that we might know not only that Christ's body was given as the price of our redemption, but that He paid a far greater and more excellent price in the suffering of His soul and spirit.

> We must learn to habitually say the right things about God and to God.

Through His willingness to suffer as our substitute, Jesus took on the sin of all mankind—the terrible and collective sins of condemned and forsaken men—with Jonah included in that lot and a prime example of it. Salvation belongs to the Lord. It is all from Him. It is not partly from you and partly from Him. It is from Him. Period. We are simply not capable of wanting Him or seeking Him on our own. It is only His grace and unmerited favor toward us that makes our deliverance possible. Salvation through God's grace is all of the Lord.

Of the many valuable lessons we learn from Jonah about prayer, five are particularly noteworthy:

1. The Language of Prayer

Language matters when we speak to God; we must learn to habitually say the right things about God and to God, for this is what keeps hope alive, especially when we find ourselves in desperate situations. Right things—true things about God are found in one place—His Word. We are always on the right side of things and in line with His will when we restate the truth found in the Bible.

2. The Perseverance of Prayer

We must keep pressing on and continue clinging to God through prayer even when the situation is desperate. He has promised us His presence and His power to overcome. He is always there and has promised never to leave us. Whatever the problem, God can solve it with His grace. Our sins are no match for His mercy. His grace is greater than our sin.

3. The Hope of Prayer

We must keep hope alive, even when we see nothing but hopelessness. The Most High God is a personal God. He sees the sparrow fall and knows the number of hairs on your head. He is the "God of *my* salvation." It is personal—for you and for me in our own specific situation—as desperate and in need of deliverance as we may be.

4. The Honesty of Prayer

We must not be afraid to be honest. It is better to be transparent in our doubt than theologically correct in our unbelief. Honest language, and the expression of doubt, despair and confusion allow what might have been a barrier to God to become a bridge to God.

5. The Persistence of Prayer

Persistence may be the most underrated virtue of one's prayer life. It is hard to persist when things appear so dark. But Jesus, who was better acquainted with darkness than anyone else, assures us that God is responsive to our persistent praying. He knows, He sees, He cares and He answers.

The God who allows the waters of life to churn with great frenzy is the same God who calms them.

GOING DEEPER

CHARACTER TRAIT:
LOVING GOD THROUGH SUFFERING WELL

"And you shall love the Lord your God with all your heart, with all your soul, with all your mind, and with all your strength . . ."
(Mark 12:30)

What It Means to "Suffer Well"

Suffering well for the cause of Christ in this life is perhaps the greatest evidence of genuine love of God. To choose to trust God and cling to Him in times of desperation, distress and suffering is a powerful testimony to the sufficiency of God, and an affirmation on the part of the one who suffers that what God allows into the life of the believer is purposeful and always intended for one's best. Loving God means placing one's unquestioning trust in His goodness in all things. According to Oswald Chambers, if anything—including the closest relationships of a disciple's life—conflict with the claims of Jesus Christ, then our Lord requires instant obedience

> It is better to be transparent in our doubt than theologically correct in our unbelief.

to Himself. This often includes the likely possibility of suffering for the gospel and for the sake of Christ—of doing things that bring one into great conflict with the forces of evil and the world. It means loss of relationships, loss of favor, loss of reputation, persecution and a host of other uncomfortable experiences in this life. It certainly requires doing things we would not normally choose to do.

Discipleship means passionate devotion to a Person—our Lord Jesus Christ. It is costly and will require sacrifice, surrender and suffering on our part. There is a vast difference between devotion to person and devotion to a cause. Our Lord never proclaimed a cause; He proclaimed personal devotion to Himself at all costs. Therefore, to be a disciple—a servant, an ambassador of His truth—is to be a devoted bondservant (one who is subservient to and entirely at the disposal of his Master; a slave) motivated by love (displayed through obedience) for the Lord Jesus, no matter the cost.

Many who call themselves Christians are not truly devoted to Jesus simply because no one on earth has this passionate love for the Lord Jesus unless the Holy Spirit gives it to Him. We may admire, respect and revere Christ, but we cannot *love* Him with all our heart, mind and soul on our own. The only One who *truly loves* the Lord Jesus is the Holy Spirit, and according to Paul, it is He who has "poured into our hearts" this very "love of God" (Romans 5:5). Whenever the Holy Spirit sees an opportunity to glorify Jesus through you, He will take your entire being and set you ablaze with glowing devotion, obedience and trust in Jesus Christ.[1]

Willingness to suffer for Christ through blind obedience and trust is a powerful testimony to the reality of God in the life of a believer. It is the supreme test of one's authentic love of God.

Eight Biblical Realities of Loving God through Suffering

1. Suffering for the cause of Christ is a certainty. Acts 14:22—". . . Through many trials and tribulations you must enter the kingdom."
2. All who suffer are forced to look for light and purpose in their pain. Only the Most High God provides light and purpose.
3. All suffering is the same in regards to two things:
   a. The intent of Satan to destroy your faith.
   b. The intent of God to strengthen and deepen your faith.
   The choice to love God or reject Him is yours.
4. God is most often rejected because of a misunderstanding of the

biblical view of suffering. Suffering is common to man, not the exception.

5. God's intention is to spread the gospel through the suffering of his servants. The testimonies of those who "suffer well" are a powerful witness to the truth of the sufficiency of the Most High God.

6. Supreme value and worship of the Most High God is on display when people see God as more valuable than anything else—more valuable than what is sacrificed or lost.

7. God must become *more* to each of us—more valuable than anything or anyone. This is the evidence of one's genuine love of God.

8. Satan's work is ultimately the work of God and His sovereignty over all things. Nothing can thwart the purposes of God.

Our testimonies to God's greatness produce a powerful aroma in which God delights. Nothing pleases Him more than to see His children bringing great glory to Him through the faith building experiences. He allows into our lives. To respond to God in humble childlike trust pleases God and brings great favor and grace to His servants. This is the blessed life—the Spirit-filled life—the life of humble surrender and sacrifice that God intends for us. Trust in God, and obedience to His plans and purposes when we do not understand is the greatest evidence of our genuine love of Him. Suffering well accomplishes incredible beauty and fruit that lasts in the heart of the servant who learns to take it as the evidence of God's love.

Suffering is often God's means of perfecting us and conforming us to the likeness of Christ. His ways are far higher and His purposes far greater than anything we can ever contrive. "Suffering produces patience, and patience produces character. And character produces hope, hope that you are finally becoming the kind of person you were always meant to become, and hope does not disappoint or make us ashamed" (Romans 5:3–5). This kind of hope leaves one fully confident and absolutely certain that God is indeed faithful, no matter what He asks of us and no matter what the assignment might cost us. His grace is sufficient for our every need. As the great pastor and author of the great hymn, *Amazing Grace*, John Newton declared: "Everything is needful that He sends; nothing is needful that He withholds!"

When you become Christ's disciple, you are no longer your own. You belong to your Master, Jesus Christ. When you go through a time of suffering, seemingly all alone, John 17 is a great way to regain your perspective on who you are and why you are experiencing intense conflict and crisis. It explains exactly why you are where you are. It is because Jesus, in His prayer to the Father before He Himself went willingly to the cross, has prayed that *you* "may be one" with the Father just as He is. Suffering well in His grace is intended to make you "one with Him."

> Suffering is common to man, not the exception.

Are you helping God to answer that prayer, or do you—like Jonah—have some other goal for your life and are therefore resistant to His ways with you? God reveals in John 17 that His purpose is not just to answer our prayers of desperation and deliverance from our suffering, but that through prayer and trust, we might come to discern His mind and His intentions in our suffering, producing through our lives a far greater impact for Him. There is one prayer that God always answers when we love Him enough to pray it for ourselves. It is the prayer of Jesus—"that they may be one just as We are one . . . ." Our suffering, therefore, is a vehicle used by God to deepen our love, devotion and oneness to God whose ways are always for our good and His glory.

Jonah's Reluctance to Love God with All His Heart

Jonah's story reveals that there were things far more important to Him than His love of God. His experience of suffering in the belly of the great fish was intended by God to expose what was so desperately wrong in his heart. And like Jonah—as long as there is something more important than God in the heart (an idol)—we will likewise be both fragile, prideful, judgmental, shallow and self-righteous. In Jonah's own prayerful words, "Those who cling to idols *forfeit the grace* that could be theirs." Whatever it is, *it must be surrendered* for it will create a stronghold of pride and an inclination to look down upon those who do not measure up (in our sinful eyes). It will also create fear, insecurity and a frantic attempt to protect oneself. Your idol becomes the basis for your happiness and if anything threatens it, you will become overwhelmed with anger, anxiety and despair. We are wise to pay attention, therefore, to the symptoms of Jonah's heart disease for we all suffer from the same deadly malady.

To reach the place of genuine love for God is to recognize all the ways that we make good things into idols and ways of saving ourselves. Genuine love for God is realized and put into action instead when we finally recognize that we live wholly by the grace of God—even to the very breath we breathe! Suffering is intended to expose our idols and get us on the right track again—living by God's grace and in His grace. Only then, with this realization, can we begin to serve the Lord effectively — not in order to get things from Him but simply out of genuine love of Him, for His own sake, just for who He is, for the simple joy of knowing and obeying Him, delighting in Him and becoming like Him. When we finally reach this foundational place, our insight and understanding begin to drain us slowly but surely of our self-righteousness and fear, making us willing to surrender and to accept our suffering for Christ, abandoning anything that might be standing in the way of His greater purposes and of our refinement and conformity to His image.

PAUSE TO PONDER

Principles for Godly Living
Loving God Through Suffering Well

1. Scripture always strengthens prayer.
2. Knowing God's word is the best insurance policy for those times in life when we find ourselves in desperate straits.

3. When we pray God's word, we can be assured we are praying His will.

4. God promises His children a way of escape in the trial that often comes through the power that is ours through His word.

5. Suffering well for the cause of Christ in this life is perhaps the greatest evidence of genuine love of God.

6. All suffering is the same in regards to two things: the intent of Satan to destroy your faith and the intent of God to strengthen your faith.

7. God's intention is to spread the gospel of His grace through the suffering of His servants.

8. The testimonies of those who "suffer well" are a powerful witness to the truth of the sufficiency of the Most High God.

9. God must become more to each of us—more valuable than anything else—more valuable than what is sacrificed or lost.

10. To respond to God in humble childlike trust pleases God and brings great favor and grace to his servants.

11. If we still have breath in our bodies, God is not finished with us!

Questions for Life Transformation

1. Describe a desperate situation God allowed in your life to get your attention and draw you back into His will and purpose. What miraculous provision did you witness in your situation that strengthened your faith in God's goodness?

2. After studying this story, how does your life measure up in regards to loving God through suffering well? How does Jonah's example challenge you to live differently? Will you ask God now for the courage to believe that whatever He allows in your life is for your good and His glory?

3. How has this story increased your understanding and appreciation of the mercy, patience, and grace of God toward you personally?

NOTE

1. Chambers, Oswald. *My Utmost For His Highest*. Westwood, Barbour and Company, Inc., 1987.

Story Two: A Recap

Jonah's Second Chance

Having begun his long journey *running from God*, Jonah, out of desperation and in a spirit of fresh humility, *ran to God* while in the belly of the sea creature through prayer. Finally re-directed to the clearly revealed will of God for his life, Jonah was now ready to *run to* Nineveh for God in order to complete the task he had originally been given. And by the undeserved favor and grace of God, Jonah finally *ran into* his faithful, patient and forgiving God. Despite God's grace of a second chance, there were additional lessons Jonah yet needed to acquire to become the prophet God intended him to be. Indeed, the process of sanctification in the life of a believer takes a lifetime but Paul assures us in Philippians, lest we lose hope: "He who began a good work in you will be faithful to complete it" (Philippians 1:6). Hallelujah! *If we still have breath in our bodies, He is not finished with us!*

With Jonah's heart *re-aligned* and his course *re–directed*, God *re–commissioned* His prophet to *return* to the assignment he had initially been called to accomplish. *The same God who allows the waters of life to churn with great frenzy is the God who calms them.* What profound grace the Father extends to His wayward children! He showers His undeserving servants with His blessing and grace for He desires to use us to extend these same blessings of grace to others in order to expand His Kingdom on earth. He is not willing that any should perish, but that all should receive His forgiveness and pardon from His most gracious hand—and that included the Ninevites!

So the word of the Lord came to Jonah a *second time*,

"Go to the great city of Nineveh and proclaim to it the message I give you."

And Jonah obeyed and went to Nineveh!

Story 3

Running With God

Jonah 3

Principle Truth:

In spite of man's rebellious nature, the Most High God is willing
that no one perish, but that all come to repentance.

Key Concepts:

Doctrine:	The Depravity of Man
Attribute of God:	The Wrath of God
Character Trait:	Loving Others through Serving

Chapter 7

Jonah's Re-Commission

In spite of man's rebellious nature, the Most High God is willing that no one perish, but that all come to repentance.

Paradox: a statement which seems opposed to common sense or contradicts itself, but is true. A form of expression that seems to be either self-contradictory or absurd.

"Mighty Deliverer, You conquered by dying—You led by serving. You lifted others by lowering Yourself. You are a paradox I will never understand. You ask me to hold on and to let go; to shed the past and to put on the future. To fix my eyes on the unseen rather than the seen and to know a love that surpasses knowledge. To lean on what I cannot prove in order to receive what I cannot earn. You invite me to stop trying so hard and be perfect instead; and when I fail—to stop feeling guilty and simply be forgiven. I want to understand You, but I can't. And when I try to wrap my mind around You, I fail. You are the mystery I will never grasp, offering a puzzling comfort I cannot live without."[1]

We've all attempted to run away from God at one time or another in our walk of faith. Perhaps that is why we can relate so well to the life of the prophet Jonah. Even the giants of the faith from time to time acted in rebellion and attempted to run from God's calling upon their lives. Abraham, Moses, Gideon, Samson and others who claimed to love God with their whole heart and who walked with God faithfully, at times ran from His purposes and ignored His calling. The tasks of eternal significance to which God calls His servants are often challenging, difficult and at times even paradoxical. Often, in our limited perspective, the assignment makes no sense at all for God's ways are mysterious, and we cannot begin to understand the impact of our obedience or the deadly consequences in the lives of countless people because of our disobedience. Nor can we begin to fathom the depth of God's great love for the lost. Therefore, *in spite of man's rebellious nature, the Most High God is willing that no one perish but that all come to repentance.*

In God's Kingdom, paradoxes abound. To be mature, we must become childlike. To make a difference for God's kingdom, we must be bolder than a lamb and freer than a slave. In God's Kingdom, fools tutor the wise, the weak lead the strong, death is swallowed by life, and love often feels like pain. Likewise, at times the assignment God ordains involves people we love to hate!

Jonah was among those who despised his God-ordained assignment and as a result, he ignored it! But God is full of love and abounding in mercy. Thus, although the logical response was for God to cast Jonah off and seek a more willing and submissive servant, in His great mercy, God chose to discipline him. Hebrews 12:5–6 states:

> "My son, do not make light of the discipline of the Lord, and
> do not lose heart and give up when you are corrected by Him.
> For the Lord disciplines those He loves."

There is a great difference between punishment and discipline. Punishment is justice for wrongdoing. Discipline is corrective with the intention of redirection and restoration. There is not one difficulty that God brings into our lives as believers that is punishment. Why is this?

Our sin—past, present and future—was punished on the cross. Every sin that a believer has committed, or will commit, or is committing has been punished through the finished work of Jesus on the cross. Perfect justice was accomplished at the cross. The *corrective discipline* of God comes with a series of sovereign nudges that bring just enough pressure to alert us to the problem and get us back on the track of righteousness and obedience. Proverbs 3:11–12 states:

> "My son, do not despise the Lord's discipline, and do not resent His rebuke, because the Lord disciplines those He loves, as a father the son he delights in."

Hebrews 12 states that if God doesn't discipline you, you are not His child. Therefore, in regard to our own children, not only do we have the right to *encourage* them into right paths when they get derailed, but we also have the responsibility and the *stewardship* as a parent to *discipline* them. Discipline comes from the heart of a loving Father and as children of a loving father, we must open our hearts to the trials and hardships so that the Lord might correct us through them and reorder our steps.

Jonah was chosen to be God's mouthpiece to the lost of Nineveh, but refused the assignment. Discipline was God's response; a series of strong, sovereign nudges intended to draw the prophet back toward obedience, back to Nineveh. God nudged him time and time again, yet he stubbornly maintained his sinful course. However, when it comes to discipline, God has options we never dreamed of. Just as Jonah obviously thought he could win this battle of the wills, God directed a great fish to Jonah's precise location, saying in essence:

> "Do you see that boat? I want you to swim next to it and when you see a big splash and a man tossed into the water, that is your lunch! Swallow it!"

Jonah lived three days and nights in that underwater cave. He wrestled with God until finally after three days of this devastating discipline and imploring God for deliverance, he was vomited out of the fish's belly and given a second chance. God's discipline is intended to get our stubborn wills into alignment with His will and His ways.

As children of the Most High God, perhaps the greatest paradox of all is that we deserve nothing and yet, we receive everything—even when we foolishly turn away from God. God is not quick to give up on His children, but disobedience comes at a great cost and often requires harsh discipline from His loving hand. Such was the case with Jonah. Nevertheless, after the course of God's severe discipline, and having been released from the prison of the great fish, Jonah was greatly humbled and far more submissive to the non-negotiable instructions of His God. Therefore, when God was satisfied with the sincerity of his sorrow, He returned to His servant a second time saying,

> "Go to the great city of Nineveh, Jonah, and proclaim to it the message I give to you."

This time Jonah obeyed immediately and set out for the godless, violent city of Nineveh. Jonah's mission included leaving his homeland and his own people to preach God's word in a foreign place—a calling that was unprecedented in the Old Testament for a prophet of God. Typical of most prophetic ministries in the Old Testament was ministry to God's own people, Israel. The fact that Jonah was called to leave his own people and carry God's message to Nineveh is yet another evidence of God's loving heart for all people.

It is, in fact, through Jonah's unique assignment that we get a glimpse—a foreshadowing—of God's greater mandate given by Jesus to all believers in every age through the Great Commission found in the Gospel of Matthew (Matthew 28:18–20). While we are not all called to be preachers, prophets or missionaries, according to Jesus, every believer is called to go. It means being willing to leave safety and security in order to share the good news of Jesus with others. This may or may not entail leaving physical and social locations, but it always means risk, sacrifice and vulnerability, and it is for every person who belongs to the Body of Christ—not just a select few. We must never forget that God is by nature a sending God. He never *calls us in* to bless us without also *sending us out* to be a blessing to others.

Thus, the one who had been "blessed" as an Israelite—a child of the covenant keeping God—was now on his way to be a blessing to the most hated of the world's people—the Ninevites. The light of Christ must be shared! The Great Commission is not optional. For Jonah and for all believers, this is always the mission. *We are blessed to be a blessing.*

GOING DEEPER

DOCTRINE: THE DEPRAVITY OF MAN

Man's State of Depravity / God's Solution in Christ

Scripture teaches that man was created in the image of God but fell into disobedience through a voluntary decision to act in defiance of God (Genesis 2 and 3). As a result, man became separated from God and therefore, spiritually dead and subject to physical death. This fallen nature was transmitted to all successive humanity, except to Jesus Christ who lived a sinless life. The blood of Jesus Christ (our sinless substitute) was God's solution to man's sinful state and depravity. His blood was shed for our redemption. Only those who receive Jesus Christ by faith are cleansed, forgiven, born of the Holy Spirit and thus become children of God. Faith alone is the condition of salvation, but good works and righteous living accompany such faith and furnish the evidence of it.

Effects of the Fall

The immediate effects of the Fall in the lives of Adam and Eve became visible initially: 1. In the loss of their boldness and joy in the presence of God, but also, 2. In the emergence of fear and shame—emotions that were before this time, foreign and unfamiliar. The effects became visible also in their: 3. Alienation from God. This separation was manifested further in: 4. The generational curse in relation to all mankind who followed Adam, but more pointedly in: 5. The expulsion of Adam and Eve from the Garden.

The Garden of Eden was the dwelling place of righteousness, union, intimacy and communion between man and God. God clearly warned that the consequences of sin would be death. Death from this point on would intervene at every point where there was life. The eventual decay of the physical body to dust in the grave is the irrefutable evidence of this curse resulting from the Fall described in Genesis 3.

> Faith alone is the condition of salvation, but good works and righteous living accompany such faith and furnish the evidence of it.

The consequences of the Fall are not limited to Adam and Eve, but extend to all those descended from them because there is a unique relationship of commonality that exists between Adam and the rest of the human race. The consequences of Adam's sin for the entire human race involved the *imputing* of his sin to all his descendants, their consequential and inevitable death, and their inheritance of a depraved nature in need of redemption. The dictionary defines the word "impute" this way: to attach to a person (in this case, Adam) responsibility for acts or injuries to another (Adam's descendants) because of a particular relationship (Father of the human race). Because of man's depraved nature, there is no one who seeks God! Therefore, apart from God's merciful intervention, man is desperately lost and without hope.

The results of the Fall are also manifest in nature itself, as the curse of the Fall works itself out even in the "groaning" of creation during this present time (Romans 8:22). Because of the Fall, only with the pain that accompanies childbirth is the world populated, and only with grueling, toilsome labor are the food, clothing and shelter necessary to sustain life provided. All of these realities are the results of Adam's transgression and his subsequent Fall.

The fact that physical death did not fall immediately upon Adam and Eve after their choice to disobey God is indicative of God's ultimate saving purpose and redemptive plan set into motion at the time Adam disobeyed and introduced sin into the human race. *It is significant that Adam was not made to bear the curse of death pronounced upon him until he had first heard the promise of a Deliverer—a Redeemer, a Savior—prophesied for the first time in Scripture in Genesis 3:15*:

> "I will put enmity between you and the woman, and between your offspring and her offspring; He (Christ, the Messiah) shall bruise your head, and you (Satan) shall bruise His heel."

After Genesis 3, the continuing effects of the Fall—the ongoing depravity of the human heart and God's need of redeeming what was lost—became the backdrop and premise of everything that follows through both individuals and nations as the struggle between good and evil unfolds. The same struggle of man's choice to obey God or to disobey God—just as in Adam's struggle—becomes the barometer of God's blessing upon a people or His curse upon them. Obedience equals blessing! The thrust of God's story in the Bible is, however, toward the future—the widening effects of sin—but nevertheless, the beautiful unfolding of God's redemptive remedy through the sending of His only son, Jesus Christ. How glorious is our salvation and the grace of our God!

Pride: The Fruit of Man's Depravity

Without question, the most telling evidence of the Fall of Genesis 3 and the resulting depravity of man's nature is the attitude of pride that so often marks human beings, both saved and unsaved alike. Pride is basically a sin of the heart and spirit, and it is the fruit of man's depravity. It is cited in the two lists of the most glaring and detestable sins recorded in the Bible. Along with the listing of sins for which God declared His judgment upon the Gentiles (those outside the covenant), Paul states further mankind's condition of depravity:

". . . they were filled with all manner of unrighteousness, evil, covetousness, malice, envy, murder, strife, deceit, and maliciousness. They are gossips, slanderers, haters of God, insolent, haughty, boastful, inventors of evil, disobedient to parents, foolish, faithless, heartless, and ruthless. Though they know God's righteous decrees, that those who practice such things deserve to die, they not only do them but give approval to those who practice them." (Romans 1:29–32)

This passage is a vivid picture of mankind without God, where depravity is blatantly on display: Pride is even uglier under the cloak of religious piety; Jesus had more to say to the religious leaders of His day concerning their legalistic pride and judgmental superiority than He ever spoke to the publicans and sinners.

Pride is the root of all sin. It affects everyone without exception. It is impossible for pride to remain internalized. It is adamant about making itself known. If not identified and confessed, it eventually reaches into every crevice of one's life, hardening the heart and rendering the person unfit for God's use. It often evidences itself in one's speech, for as Jesus said, "What comes out of the mouth comes from the heart, and boasting is the result."

Pride is one of the seven things that the Lord God hates (Proverbs 6:17). It was the pride of Satan (Lucifer) by which he aspired to be "like God" that cast him out of the heavens along with one third of the angels. It is said by two different biblical writers that God opposes the proud, but gives grace to the humble (James 4:6; 1 Peter 5:5). Perhaps the words of Mary, mother of Jesus, in her hymn of praise to the Most High God best summarizes the attitude of God toward pride: "His mighty arm does tremendous things! *How He scatters the proud and haughty ones!* He has taken princes from their thrones and exalted the lowly" (Luke 1:51–52).

God always has a purpose for one's brokenness, and God's plans are always ahead of the schemes of Satan. Brokenness is an excellent means of shattering one's pride and awakening humility and the awareness of one's need of God. Thus, God often allows the enemy to do his worst in order to shake everything in need of shaking. There are five purposes for shaking an object: 1. To bring it close to its foundation; 2. To remove what is dead; 3. To harvest what is ripe; 4. To awaken; and 5. To unify or mix together so it can no longer be separated. Heart attitudes rooted in selfishness and pride must be purged by God, if one is to be used for His purposes. Jonah's pride as well as the pride of Nineveh were both in need of shaking.

Pride and the Prophet Jonah

In the story of Jonah, the pride of both God's prophet and the pride of the Ninevite people were on display. The pride of Jonah was rooted in his ugly religious piety and feelings of superiority while the pride of Nineveh came from the dark forces of pagan humanism, ignorance and alienation from God. Make no mistake, both extremes are deadly serious and offensive to a holy God. Beware of pride. It seeks to steal, to kill and to destroy the great purposes of the Most High God.

My Name is Pride
By Beth Moore[2]

"My name is Pride
I cheat you of your God-given destiny . . .
Because you demand your own way.

I cheat you of contentment . . .
Because you "deserve better than this."

I cheat you of knowledge . . .
Because you already know it all.

I cheat you of healing . . .
Because you are too full of me to forgive.

I cheat you of holiness . . .
Because you refuse to admit when you are wrong

I cheat you of vision . . .
Because you'd rather look in the mirror than out a window

I cheat you of genuine friendship . . .
Because nobody's going to know the real you.

I cheat you of love . . .
Because real romance demands sacrifice.

I cheat you of greatness in heaven . . .
Because you refuse to wash another's feet on earth.

I cheat you of God's glory . . .
Because I convince you to seek your own.

My name is Pride. I am a cheater.
You like me because you think I'm always looking out for you.
Untrue. I'm looking to make a fool of you.
God has so much for you, I admit, but don't worry,
if you stick with me, you will never know."

PAUSE TO PONDER

Principles for Godly Living
The Depravity of Man

1. We cannot underestimate the impact of our disobedience in the lives of countless people.
2. God disciplines His children as a Father in order to correct us and reorder our steps.
3. God's discipline is intended to get our stubborn wills into alignment with His will and ways.

4. Because God is by nature a sending God, He never calls us *in* to bless us without also sending us *out* to be a blessing to others.

5. Brokenness is an excellent means of shattering pride and awakening humility.

6. God always warns before sending His judgment.

Questions for Life Application

1. Share an example of a "paradoxical surprise" from God that you experienced as a result of your obedience to a difficult assignment you were reluctant to fulfill? How did the experience change your understanding of the principle: obedience equals blessing?

2. Share an experience when your pride got in the way of God's revealed purpose. What consequences followed and what might you still need to do to rid your heart of this deadly vice?

3. From this story we learn that God's discipline comes from the heart of a loving Father whose intention is to correct us and reorder our steps. Share a time when you experienced God's discipline in your life. How did God's discipline correct your steps and realign your life to His purposes?

4. Having studied the story of Jonah, how has your understanding of the doctrine of depravity changed? Explore some of the ways man's depravity is on display within the culture of today. Praise God for His remedy for our hopeless condition, which is salvation through Jesus Christ.

5. Explore some ways that pride cheats us from God's best. Why is it so important that we understand the source of pride?

NOTES

1. James, Steven. *A Heart Exposed*. Grand Rapids, Revel, 2009.

2. Moore, Beth. *Living Free: Learning to Pray God's Word*. Nashville, Lifeway Press, 2015.

Chapter 8

God's Command to Nineveh

---

*In spite of man's rebellious nature, the Most High God is willing
that no one perish, but that all come to repentance.*

Travel to the city of Nineveh was no easy task for Jonah, particularly
after the traumatic ordeal at sea. Physically, the journey required every
ounce of his remaining strength for it spanned some 500 miles mostly
through enemy territory. Spiritually, the assignment was even more challenging. God's specific instruction was for Jonah to parrot a redundant
message over and over in countless repetitions as he walked through the
streets of the great capital city of the Assyrian Empire . . .

"Yet 40 days and Nineveh is to be overthrown!
Yet 40 days and Nineveh will be destroyed!
Judgment is coming!
God's judgment is at the door!
Nineveh is soon to be destroyed by Almighty God and over-
thrown!"

Jonah was allowed no latitude with regard to the message, and like
a broken record, he shouted the words relentlessly to any and all who
would listen. These were words of warning from God meant specifically

for Nineveh. Because the Most High God is a merciful God, He always warns before sending His judgment. Jonah was His instrument to wake the people up from their violent ways and call them to repentance.

God's words were alive and powerful as Jonah preached them! The prophet's simple sermon was neither eloquent nor lengthy, but delivered in the power of the Spirit of God. It was, therefore, profound and life-changing, and the most amazing thing was the response that began to take place as Jonah meandered through the city streets meeting person after person. The hardness upon empty faces began to melt away into a strange curiosity followed by an eagerness to hear more. Before he knew it, Jonah realized that people up and down the city streets were now following him, listening to him, receiving his message and even believing the message of imminent judgment he so forcefully declared.

The results were nothing short of a miracle! One of the cruelest nations in all of world history heard a message of warning from a servant of the Most High God (a previously unwilling one), and in mass, the people repented of their wickedness! The entire city, from king to pauper and yes, even to the animals of their fields, all were humbled and repentant before a holy God. How could such a thing happen? What made the difference in the mindset of the people from one normal day to the next? Precisely what awakened them out of their slumber? What caused them to see, really see, with such clarity their own depravity before a holy God? What could possibly have caused the change?

It was a paradox—one of those strange occurrences that only God can orchestrate but are so commonplace in the Kingdom of God. A man who was a Jew, whom Ninevites hated and who hated them—a despised enemy—walked directly into their city and began preaching God's powerful truth and the reality of coming judgment. Clearly the widespread acceptance of Jonah's message was miraculous, for before this time, there had been no witness to the truth in this dark and wicked place. Hearing the truth for the very first time, particularly through God's prophet, produced an overwhelming harvest of repentant people. What began to transpire throughout the city, therefore, was unprecedented. An "Awakening" of sorts took place in every nook and cranny of the city.

> "For the word of God is living and active, sharper than any double-edged sword, it penetrates even to dividing soul and spirit, joints and marrow; it judges the thoughts and attitudes of the heart. Nothing in all creation is hidden from God's sight. *Everything is uncovered and laid bare before the eyes of Him to whom we must give account.*" (Hebrews 4:12–13)

To Jonah's shock, the people neither laughed, scoffed, nor laid hands on him. They responded! The Hebrew word for "repent" ("shub"—to turn) occurs four times in verses 8–10 of the text, and this is indeed the central message of Jonah 3. Against all expectation, the violent people of Nineveh put on sackcloth, a sign of mass repentance—from the greatest to the least—from the top to the bottom of the social spectrum. Astounding! How could this have happened? And examining the biblical record, was this a *genuine* act of repentance as God's word explains it?

It is quite interesting and in fact providential, but historians concur that about the time of Jonah's mission, the powerful empire of Assyria experienced a series of devastating natural disasters and deadly pestilence—all of which were seen as omens of far worse things to come. Jonah arrived in Nineveh on the heels of several of these catastrophic events. Secular history records that in the year 765 BC, a devastating plague of unknown origin took the lives of a large segment of the population. In 763 BC, a total eclipse occurred leaving the people in awe of an unexplained terrifying darkness occurring in the middle of the day. And once again in 759 BC, another plague of unknown origin swept through the city wiping out great numbers.

These bizarre, unexplainable occurrences were meaningful events God used in a culture where superstition and the occult were predominant features. Could it be that this was God's way of preparing the hearts of the Ninevites for Jonah's arrival and his sobering message of certain judgment to come? These unusual events would surely have made both rulers and subjects unusually attuned to the timely message of a strange-looking visiting prophet. Essentially Nineveh—a people proud, powerful and invincible, ceased (at least for a time) to be that nation the entire ancient world knew her to be. In the place of her former prideful superiority, humility began to surface from the greatest to the least. It was indeed a dramatic change!

Although there was indeed an "Awakening," we must be careful to note that the Bible gives no indication that the Ninevites came into a covenant relationship with the God of Israel. The word the Ninevite people used when speaking of "God" was the general term "Elohim" rather than the personal covenant name "Yahweh"—the name the Lord used with His people Israel. There is no mention of the residents of Nineveh forsaking their pagan gods and idols. We are not told anywhere that they offered sacrifices to the Lord, nor is there any rite of circumcision mentioned—the sign of the covenant people of the Most High God. A deeper look into exactly what happened in the Ninevite "Awakening" is needful.

The king of Nineveh understood God (Elohim) to be saying that each citizen of the city must "*forsake his evil way and the violence* that he planned toward others" (3:8). Nineveh was blatantly guilty of exploitation, violence and social injustice of indescribable proportions. In fact, Assyria's cruelty and imperialism were condemned strongly by other Hebrew prophets as well (Isaiah 10:31; Nahum 3:1,19). Jonah's call for Nineveh to repent of her wicked oppression and injustice is the same message other biblical prophets spoke to similar pagan nations. In the Old Testament when an Israelite prophet addressed a pagan nation, the condemnation was typically targeted at moral and social wickedness. This is exactly what Jonah did as well. His message focused on the city's social practices, their deeds (3:10) their social injustice, and the call was for them to change their ways (3:4) in regard to their social interactions, their society, their culture.

The Assyrians slaughtered, enslaved people and oppressed the poor.

The nation was renowned among surrounding nations for its injustice, imperialism and oppression. The truth of the matter? This exploitation and abuse was eating away at the very fabric of Nineveh's society. Individuals were cruel toward one another, and social relationships were poisoned. The King himself spoke forth words admonishing the people to forsake their wicked ways.

> "Let every person forsake . . . the violence that he plans toward others." (v. 8)

The wealthy enslaved the poor while the poor struck back through violent crime and aggressive retaliation. Therefore, "repentance from the greatest to the least" was an indication of the beginnings of an "Awakening" to the reality of their depravity—the beginnings of the Ninevite's awareness of their wickedness and a change of direction in the way these people were living among one another; a turning from such evil practices to good will, peace and social justice. Essentially the city shifted in their actions from depravity toward the righteous ways of the Most High God. They heeded Jonah's message, and the Most High God met them more than half way! The people turned to God in hopes that it was not too late for Him to hear them. *In spite of man's rebellious nature, the Most High God is willing that no one perish but that all come to repentance.*

Nevertheless, the biblical text does not state that God sent Jonah to Nineveh with the purpose of converting the people into a saving, covenant relationship with Him. He was sent simply to warn them of their evil, violent behavior and the inevitable consequences certain to follow if they did not change course. It is important to note that changing social behavior is *not* sufficient for salvation. Faith, repentance and an atoning sacrifice must be present for genuine salvation. In the Old Testament, this was accomplished through the Israelite sacrificial system, and in the New Testament by the blood of the perfect sacrifice, Jesus Christ at the Cross.

> Changing social behavior is *not* sufficient for salvation.

God's response to Nineveh's "repentance" is particularly instructive. Though the people of Nineveh did not forsake their idols or make sacrifices to Him, God, in great mercy, relented from His threat to destroy the city. For the time being, God expressed His favor in response to the city's intention and effort at social reform. Therefore, although positive reform did take place within the society and culture, *there is no evidence of genuine conversion to saving faith* in the Most High God. There was a coming together of warring classes and contentious individuals within the Assyrian culture in order to bring about social healing and a more just society. Yet, the radical change was the result of a preaching and prophetic ministry that testified to the truth of the wrath of Israel's God—the Most High God. What we find in Nineveh's response to Jonah's message is a city that was now willing to seek social reform and make changes regarding their violent behavior toward one another. God, however, also directed Jonah to tell these people about a God of wrath who indeed punishes sin.

The commentator Jacque Ellul in his excellent commentary, *The Judgment of Jonah,* states:

> "Jonah was not free to select for himself what he would say to men. He did not go to them to tell them about his personal experiences . . . He did not decide the content of his preaching. Thus, our witness is fast bound to the Word of God. The greatest saint can say nothing of value unless it is based solely on God's word."[1]

What God's message through Jonah teaches is that there is a divine link between preaching the Word boldly without fear, and justice and care for the poor. The two are inseparable. In the days of Isaiah, Israelite society was marked by similar vices: greedy exploitation of the poor and abuse of power rather than generosity, peaceful service and cooperation. These conditions inevitably led to social breakdown and the eventual collapse of the kingdom of Israel. Isaiah states:

> "Through the wrath of the Lord of hosts, the land is scorched,

and the people are like fuel for the fire; no one spares another . . . they devour . . . but are not satisfied . . . Manasseh devours Ephraim, and Ephraim devours Manasseh . . ." (Isaiah 9:19–21)

The misery and social breakdown, the economic and political "devouring" of one another, along with the inner emptiness and discontent all of it brings is actually the outworking of God's wrath. Without understanding the reality of the wrath of God, it is impossible to fully understand why so many societies, empires, institutions and individual lives break down. Romans 1:18 states this reality in no uncertain terms:

"For God does not overlook sin, and the wrath of God is revealed from heaven against all ungodliness and unrighteousness of men who in their wickedness, suppress and stifle the truth."

In a similar thought, Alec Motyer (qtd. in Keller 114) states:

"In a world created by a good God, evil and injustice are inherently self-destructive."[2]

Therefore, the disintegration of a society is indeed the outward expression of God's holy wrath against sin. He presides over the cause and effect processes that He Himself has built into creation, so they are expressions of His holy rule of the world. God created the world so that cruelty, greed and exploitation have natural, eroding consequences that are manifestations of His anger toward evil.

Thus, Jonah was sent to expose the moral disintegration, and his method of exposure was the use of the sword of the Spirit that is the Word of God. From the reaction recorded in Jonah 3, we see that truly the Word of God *is* sharper than a two-edged sword. It obviously accomplished the purpose for which it was sent!

ATTRIBUTE OF GOD: WRATH

A Definition

Wrath is defined as "the emotional response to perceived wrong and injustice," often translated as anger, indignation, vexation or irritation. Both humans and God express wrath; however, there is vast difference between them. God's wrath is holy and always justified; man's wrath is never holy and rarely justified.

God's Wrath in the Old Testament

The wrath of God is the divine response to human sin and disobedience. Without question, Israel's idolatry was most often the occasion for divine wrath. Psalm 78:56–66 states:

> "Yet, they tempted and rebelled against the Most High God and did not keep His testimonies. They turned back and acted unfaithfully like their fathers; they were twisted like a warped bow that will not respond to the archer's aim. For they provoked Him to anger with their high places devoted to idol worship and moved Him to jealousy with their carved images. When God heard this, He was filled with righteous wrath, and utterly rejected Israel, (greatly hating her ways)."

The wrath of God is consistently directed toward those who do not follow His will. The Old Testament prophets often wrote of a day in the future when the "day of wrath" from heaven would fall (Zephaniah 1:14–15). God's wrath against sin and disobedience is perfectly justified because His plan for mankind is holy and perfect, just as God Himself is holy and perfect. In mercy, God provided a way to gain divine favor: *repentance*—turning from sin by confession and a willingness to change course. Only repentance and a genuine humbling of the heart turns God's wrath away from the sinner. To reject that perfect plan is to reject God's love, mercy, grace and favor and thus, incur His righteous judgment.

Wrath in the New Testament

The New Testament also supports the concept of the Most High God as a God of wrath who judges sin. The story of the rich man and Lazarus (Luke 16:19–31) is only one of many examples from the lips of Jesus Christ of the judgment of God and serious consequences of that judgment for the unrepentant sinner.

John 3:36 states:

> "Whoever believes in the Son has eternal life, but whoever rejects the Son will not see life, for *God's wrath remains on him.*"

The one who believes in the Son will not suffer *God's wrath* for his sin because the Son took God's wrath upon Himself when He died in our place on the cross (Romans 5:6–11). Those who do not believe in the Son, who do not receive Him as Savior, will be judged on the day of wrath.

> "Because of your callous stubbornness and unrepentant heart, you are deliberately storing up wrath for yourself on the day of wrath when God's righteous judgment will be revealed. He will pay back to each person according to his deeds: to those who by persistence in doing good seek glory, honor, and immortality, He will give the gift of eternal life. But for those who are selfishly ambitious, self-seeking, disobedient to the truth, and responsive to wickedness, there will be wrath and indignation."(Romans 2:5–9)

God alone is able to avenge because His vengeance is perfect and holy, whereas man's wrath is sinful, opening him up to demonic influence that always reaps evil and destruction. For the believer in Christ, anger and wrath are inconsistent with the new nature, which is the very nature of Christ Himself. To realize freedom from the domination of wrath, the believer needs the Holy Spirit to sanctify and cleanse his heart of feelings of wrath, vengeance and anger. Romans 8 declares victory over this particular sin in the life of the one who chooses to live in the power of the Spirit. Philippians 4:4–7 tells us that the mind controlled by the Spirit of God is filled with peace:

> "Rejoice in the Lord always; again I will say, rejoice! Let your gentle spirit be known to all people. The Lord is near. Do not be anxious or worried about anything, but in everything by prayer and petition with thanksgiving, continue to make your requests known to God. And the peace of God that transcends all understanding will stand guard over your hearts and your minds in Christ Jesus."

The wrath of God is a fearsome and terrifying thing. Only those who have been covered by the blood of Christ shed for us on the cross can be assured that God's wrath will never fall on them. "Since we have now been justified by His blood, how much more shall we be saved from God's wrath through Him!" (Romans 5:9).[3]

Five Truths About the Wrath of God[4]

1. God's Wrath is Just

It has become common for many to argue that the God of the Old Testament is a moral monster that is by no means worthy of our worship. However, biblical authors have no such problem. In fact, God's wrath is said to be in perfect accord with God's justice and His goodness. God's wrath, then, operates in proportion to human sinfulness. Proverbs 24:12 says: "If you say, 'Behold, we did not know this,' does not He who weighs the heart perceive it? Does not He who keeps watch over your soul know it, and will He not repay man according to his work?" J.I. Packer summarizes: "God's wrath in the Bible is never capricious, self-indulgent, irritable, or a morally ignoble thing that human anger so often is. It is, instead, a right and necessary reaction to objective moral evil."[5]

2. God's Wrath is to be Feared

God's wrath is to be feared because all have sinned and fallen short of the glory of God (Romans 3:23). God's wrath is to be feared because we are justly condemned sinners apart from Christ (Romans 5:1). God's wrath is to be feared because He is powerful enough to do precisely what He promises (Jeremiah 32:17). God's wrath is to be feared because God promises eternal punishment apart from Christ (Matthew 25:46).

3. God's Wrath is consistent in the Old and New Testaments

It is common to think of the Old Testament God as mean, harsh and wrath-filled, and the God of the New Testament as kind, patient and loving. Neither of these portraits are representative of Scripture's teaching. We find fearful descriptions of the wrath of God in both Testaments. A few examples follow:

A. "Behold the storm of the Lord! Wrath has gone forth, a whirling tempest; it will burst upon the head of the wicked." (Jeremiah 30:23)

B. "The Lord is a jealous and avenging God; the Lord is avenging and wrathful; the Lord takes vengeance on His adversaries and keeps wrath for His enemies." (Nahum 1:2)

Although God seems at times to give evil people a long rope before He pulls them up short, what has been reaped will indeed be sown. The wages of sin is death (evidenced through God's judgment and wrath). God did eventually destroy Nineveh. His wrath did indeed fall upon this evil nation. 40 years after Jonah visited Nineveh, Assyria's short-lived "repentance" was long passed, and the wicked nation invaded Israel and conquered the capital city of Samaria in 722 BC. Because of Israel's idolatry, God used Assyria to literally take His people, Israel, into captivity. What goes around, comes around, and in 640 BC God inspired the prophet Nahum to announce that Assyria's days were numbered. This time, there would be no prolonged mercy. The world's most ruthless nation was utterly destroyed as God's wrath fell upon this ancient nation. (See the Old Testament minor prophet, Nahum.)

C. "For the wrath of God is revealed from heaven against all ungodliness and unrighteousness of men, who by their unrighteousness suppress the truth." (Romans 1:18)

D. "From His mouth comes a sharp sword with which to strike down the nations and He will rule them with a rod of iron. He will tread the winepress of the fury of the wrath of God, the Almighty." (Revelation 19:15)

4. God's Wrath Is His Love In Action Against Sin

God is love, and God does all things for His glory. He loves His glory above all; therefore, God rules the world in such a way that brings Himself maximum glory. This means that God must act justly and judge sin (by responding with wrath); otherwise, God would not be God. God's love for His glory motivates His wrath against sin. God's love for His own glory is a most sobering reality and not good news for sinners. It is after all, "a fearful thing to fall into the hands of the living God" (Hebrews 10:31).

5. God's Wrath is Satisfied in Christ

Here is the Good News! "Christ Jesus came into the world to save sinners" (1 Timothy 1:15). Because of Christ, God can rightly call sinners justified. As Romans 3:26 states: "It was to demonstrate His righteousness at the present time, so that He would be just and the One who justifies those who have faith in Jesus and rely confidently on Him as Savior." God has done what we could not do, and He has done what we did not deserve. "There is, therefore, now no condemnation for those who are in Christ" (Romans 8:1).

God's Wrath in the Book of Jonah

God refused to allow Jonah to remain undisturbed in his wrong attitudes and behavioral patterns. He sent a storm and a fish to allow him the grace of a second chance. God is too holy and too loving to either destroy Jonah or allow him to remain as he was. It is no different for each of us. As for Nineveh, the book of Jonah shows not only that justice was important to God, but also that the preaching of repentance and the understanding of His holy wrath against sin were equally important issues to be conveyed. According to Dr. Timothy Keller in his book, *The Prodigal Prophet*, understanding these two concepts is like two wings of an airplane.[6] Both are necessary and one leads to the other. The point? We must serve the needs of our neighbor even if he or she does not share our faith. All social problems stem from alienation from God and

> All social problems stem from alienation from God and His principles.

His principles. While preaching repentance is indeed fundamental, doing justice must be inseparably attached to it. The Old Testament prophet Isaiah states that if we do not care for the poor, then we are honoring God with our lips while our hearts are far from Him (Isaiah 29:13).

PAUSE TO PONDER

Principles for Godly Living
God's Wrath

1. Changing social behavior is *not* sufficient for salvation. Faith, repentance and an atoning sacrifice must be present.
2. There is a divine link between preaching the Word boldly without fear and practicing social justice and care for the poor.
3. The disintegration of a society is the outward expression of God's holy wrath against sin.

4. God created the world so that cruelty, greed and exploitation have natural, eroding consequences that are manifestations of His anger toward evil.

5. Repentance and a genuine humbling of the heart turn God's wrath away from the sinner.

6. The wrath of God is a fearsome and terrifying thing.

7. Only those covered by the blood of Christ can be assured that God's wrath will never fall on them.

8. All social problems stem from alienation from God and His principles.

Questions for Life Application

1, The "Awakening" in Nineveh was not considered a genuine conversion to saving faith. It was merely social reform, and a turning away from violence and brutality (Jonah 3:8). Why is it important for us to see the difference between genuine salvation and social reform?

2. What evidence of the wrath of God is clearly apparent in our culture today? How does understanding God's wrath through this story allow you to see that God is in control of all things—even the deterioration of a society or nation?

NOTES

1. Ellul, Jacque. *The Judgment of Jonah*. Grand Rapids, Eerdmans, 1971.

2. Keller, Timothy. *The Prodigal Prophet: Jonah and the Mystery of God's Mercy*. New York, Viking, 2018.

3. "What is the Biblical Understanding of the Wrath of God?" *Got Questions*, https://www.gotquestions.org/wrath-of-God.html. Accessed 27 February 2020.

4. Scheumann, Joseph. "Five Truths About the Wrath of God." *Desiring God*, https://www.desiringgod.org/articles/five-truths-about-the-wrath-of-god. Accessed 6 March 2014.

5. Packer, J.I. *Knowing God*. Downers Grove, InterVarsity Press, 1973.

6. Keller. *The Prodigal Prophet*.

Chapter 9

Jonah's Effect Upon Nineveh

In spite of man's rebellious nature, the Most High God is willing that no one perish, but that all come to repentance.

It is important to understand that there are no incidental or accidental things in the life of the believer. God is constantly working on multiple levels. He was working in the life of Jonah, in the life of the sailors, and in the lives of the Ninevites—simultaneously.

The Most High God carefully orchestrated every event that took place preparing Jonah for the specific assignment awaiting him in Nineveh. He was thrown overboard by sailors who determined that he was indeed the cause of their great troubles. The pagan sailors all witnessed Jonah's "death" as he crashed into the sea and was swallowed by the huge fish. Eventually as the sailors returned to shore after their harrowing experience at sea, they surely declared to everyone a chronicle of the most unusual events they had together experienced—the violent storm, and the strange and troubled man responsible for it all.

The logical explanation of what had happened to the man responsible was that Jonah was surely dead! It was humanly impossible for anyone to have survived such catastrophic events! Only through the supernatural orchestrations and the hand of the Most High God could Jonah have lived through this ordeal. But . . . God miraculously preserved Jonah's life, giving him yet a second chance to fulfill his original assignment. Therefore, unbeknownst to the sailors, Jonah was very much alive and now walking the streets of the capital city of the Assyrian Empire with God's sobering message of imminent judgment. The people of Nineveh, from great to small were remarkably receptive; they believed Jonah and for one reason: into their wicked, godless city walked a resurrected man!

Often people come to repentance when they witness a quality of life that is different and unexplainable in human experience—the same quality of "new life" Jonah now displayed. Not only did the receptivity and the "Awakening" of the Ninevites come about from the power-fully spoken Word of God, but Jonah himself was a powerful *living* testimony of the message, walking among the people and proclaiming the truth of his God in person. The life of this strange prophet had been disciplined, corrected, preserved and sent to this city to accomplish God's assignment. He had been miraculously delivered from certain death by the hand of the Most High God; he was indeed a *resurrected* spectacle for all to see. His very appearance captured the attention of all who crossed his path before he spoke even a word.

> There are no incidental or accidental things in the life of the believer.

By God's providence, everything about Jonah was intentional—his message, his actions, even his appearance. As an aftermath of his time inside the fish, the acids from the gastric juices of the fish pouring onto him in the attempt to digest this strange meal caused Jonah's skin to manifest a whitish bleached-looking color. To add to this abnormality in his appearance, what was left of his balding hair was now a white wiry mess making him quite wild-looking! His appearance alone produced curiosity and stares from everyone commanding their undivided attention! Thus, out of nowhere walking the city streets was an odd, white skinned, disheveled man shouting about imminent judgment—and wonder of all wonders—everyone was listening! From the reports of the sailors upon their return to the port, there was no question that Jonah was dead, but to everyone's amazement here in Nineveh, he was very much alive fulfilling the assignment God originally ordained for him. *In spite of man's rebellious nature, the Most High God is willing that no one perish but that all come to repentance.*

It matters not how one looks on the outside as long as the resurrection life of Christ is at work inside the heart. Jonah marched through Nineveh stopping three times each day to preach his simple but powerfully penetrating message of God's wrath soon to overtake the nation. The people responded visibly by clothing themselves in sackcloth and ashes, a sign of deep mourning and sorrow. Their expression of grief went so far as to dress even the beasts of their fields in these garments as a sign that they indeed believed the message and had understood it to be true. Strange thing, but the city, the countryside, the people and all the animals together formed an incredible portrait of widespread *national sorrow.*

The truth of God is a powerful weapon, but the truth of the spoken Word accompanied by a transformed life is doubly profound and full of potential impact upon the lives of others. The sword of God's Spirit pierced through the darkness of Nineveh and touched the hardened hearts of the world's cruelest people. Jonah was the messenger—reluctant and disobedient to begin with, but after God's discipline, the one with a front row seat to witness God's resurrection power not only in his own life but now in the extraordinary reactions of the Ninevites surrounding him.

GOING DEEPER

CHARACTER TRAIT: LOVING OTHERS THROUGH SERVING

"And you shall love the Lord your God with all your heart, and with all your soul and with all your strength. And *you shall love your neighbor as yourself.* There is no other commandment greater than these." (Mark 12:30–31)

Loving Your Neighbor

If we are truly interested in expressing our love of God by surrendering our will to Him and suffering well for His glory as we learned from Stories 1 and 2, then the natural *evidence of our love of God* will be a *focus on others*—on those people God providentially places in our lives—our "neighbors." So often, we prefer anything but the complications that come with human relationships and interaction. We reason with thoughts such as:

"I'll tithe. I'll witness. I'll even teach—but love *that* neighbor? I don't think You know my neighbor very well, Lord. How about suggesting something else?"

And Christ would reply:

"No, the place to start loving Me with all your heart, soul and strength is by loving your neighbor." (*Yes! That neighbor!*)

With Jesus Christ as our example, we are commanded to love our "neighbor" regardless of socio-economic background, personality issues, race, color or any other so called "defining" criteria we may attach to our "reluctance" or resistance. We do not have to like people to love them. In fact, they may indeed be unlovable because few people have ever cared about them. Perhaps they have known only abuse in their troubled lives. Our love may be the beginning of a transformation or an open door in their lives—an open door to God and a new way of life. We must begin to see that it is our privilege to be what Christ would be to them. We are His hands, His feet, His voice, His heart. We are called to love our neighbor by being a source of caring, compassion and concern, and all is to be done to the glory of God.

The Meaning of Loving Your Neighbor

The essence of our love for others goes back to the meaning used in the first part of Jesus' command to "love God" first with all your soul, heart and mind. Our love for our neighbor carries the same idea as that of yielding, surrendering or giving. But because it is to be exercised toward other people, it carries a different kind of application than our love of God. Whereas loving God means surrendering to His will, loving others means to yield to their needs—to be others-oriented as a reflection and evidence of our love for God. God's love actualizes itself in two dimensions. There is first a God-given sensitivity to our neighbor's need, and secondly, there must be sacrifice on their behalf.

We need not look far to see that the world has a need—it is hopelessly lost in sin and unable to help itself. Romans 5:8 says: "But God clearly shows and proves His own love for us, by the fact that while we were still sinners, Christ died for us." The "us" in Romans 5:8 is defined as we who are sinners. We must remember where we once were, and the grace of God that delivered us! Being first sensitive to our own need, Christ sacrificed from His abundant resources to meet our need. Christ died for us while we were yet sinners. That sacrifice, unlike any other, was the necessary outgrowth of God's choice to express His love toward us. Likewise, our love cannot be complete if both components, *sensitivity* to others and their needs, and *sacrifice* for others are not in place. When we understand love in this way, it demands that we reverse the tendency of our flesh to be selfish and prideful, and begin to live with an others-first attitude. Philippians 2:2–8 is worthy of memorization in this regard.

> ". . . Each of you should look not only to your own interests, but also the interests of others. Your attitude should be the same as that of Christ Jesus; who, being in very nature God, did not consider equality with God something to be grasped, but made himself nothing, taking the very nature of a servant, being made in human likeness . . ."

Christ modeled His love for others with His time and talents, and so must we. He took time with the sick, the children, the disciples and even the Pharisees—His worst enemies. He invested His time in teaching them, healing them, encouraging and reproving them. His eternal talents were spent on their behalf. We all have an inventory of resources in our lives.

We have time to give, talents to share, a listening ear, a comforting smile, a hug, a bag of groceries, a meal, prayers of intercession, and just a simple, "I love you!" Those are all within easy grasp of every believer and are the evidence of practical love that, through Christ, we each possess. Our love of God is manifested, therefore, in these acts of kindness shown to others.

Our pride and selfish preferences often rob us of the love Christ so desires that we extend to others, especially those not like us. Christ gave up many of His heavenly prerogatives to love us. When love is sacrificial, it demonstrates its true depth. What we are willing to give up for someone else reflects the quality of our love for them. Love is most difficult to give when it demands that we sacrifice a preference, a liberty, or anything that will cost us something. Unfortunately, intolerance and imposing our prejudice upon others can divide and defeat even the best efforts in advancing the cause of Christ in the world. God tells us that our love for others is the one thing that lifts us above all the pettiness. It is simply a matter of making our love of others more important than our pride, our personal privilege, and our preference or liberty.

> Love is most difficult to give when it demands that we sacrifice a preference, a liberty, or anything that will cost us something.

The Command to Judge Not

People who are bound by systems or laws are prone to criticism and spiritually devalue those who do not fit their code. Romans 14:9–12 demands that one give up his judgmental ways, and stop using his own preferences as a spiritual whipping post for others. There is only one thing that makes us truly distinct in a self-serving, self-gratifying world, and that is a Christlike sense of concern and compassion for others that is willing to sacrifice for the benefit of another. Only those who themselves have been to the foot of the cross and who have been loved by God unconditionally have the capacity to consistently reach out to others for the sake of loving God. It is the way the world will know we are His.

We are to be known as Christ followers by our love. God's people operating within a caring community (with an intense interest in the needs of others) generates a powerful attraction to Christ. In a world becoming more self-centered, people are searching for someone who will reach out and show them a way of life that matters—that has purpose— not just a meaningless existence from day to day.

A church that really cares will target the lost who are longing for love and hope. They will look for opportunities and open doors to meet the needs of the lost with the intention of ultimately sharing the life-giving message of God's truth. It was often said of the first-century church, "Oh, how they love one another." They expressed their love through their deeds. Love within the community of God's people cuts an important pathway for effective evangelism. The unity of God's people in a community of faith is itself a sign of the Spirit's presence and power. People must know we care before we can be trusted with a platform to speak.

The Great Challenge of Loving our Neighbor

Exactly who then is my neighbor? According to Christ, your neighbor is anyone who enters the arena of your existence—strangers, the lost, friends, family, and those who live nearby as well as those who live far away. The Pharisees sought to get Christ's opinion as to who their neighbor was, and He included even one's enemies as He told the Story

> People must know we care before we can be trusted with a platform to speak.

of the Good Samaritan. In that parable Christ illustrates that anyone in need, friend or foe, is a neighbor. He concluded that neighborly love is showing sacrificial mercy on anyone who has a need and whom we can help.

Integrating the mind of Christ and His example of loving others into our existence (the attitude that is both sensitive and sacrificial to the needs of others) is a great challenge that will indeed inconvenience us and move us out of our comfort zone. It is impossible to love others without getting our hands dirty! In summary, the challenges of loving others must be faced on three fronts: 1. the challenge from within, 2. the challenge from our culture, and 3. the challenge of our neighbor himself.

1. The Challenge from Within

Perhaps the greatest obstacle that lies in the way of loving others is as close as our own heart! It is extremely difficult to love others well because of our sinful bent toward self. All sin begins with doing what the self wants to do for itself. The flesh always sends the arrows of one's energy back toward "me" so that I seek to serve the big "I"—my needs, my freedom, my preferences, my convenience, my comfort, my desires. Christ's way is the opposite. It means taking the impact of my resources, my energies and my possessions, and only through the Spirit's power redirecting them toward those outside my life and around me. The challenge from within of self and pride will always be a voice pulling us in a direction toward self—never toward others.

2. The Challenge from Without

The voices of our culture dramatically contradict the kingdom understanding of both ourselves and others. The prevailing ethic of today's world begins with "me." Self-fulfillment, self-help, self-realization is the central motivation for most. Tragically, believers bring this deadly baggage on board as they begin their life-long pilgrimage with Christ.

Although we claim to be reflections of His love, we remain for the most part, committed to "me." Therefore, if "I" am all-important, then others are not as important as I. This mindset involves the thought that people exist to bring joy to me, to help make me successful, to provide for my social acceptance and encouragement. Others are the means by which I get rid of my loneliness—the people I am seen with—and thus, they become that which I climb on, play with, and push out of the way.

If we see people as a means to our ends of gaining more, we will use them, deceive them, and misrepresent them—all to get and gain for ourselves. The result? Our neighbor becomes neglected, used, abused and pushed aside. This is the way of the world over which Satan the "Prince of the Power of the air" rules. The voice of the world will always tell you that life is about *you* . . . becoming your best self and living your best life! Sound familiar?

Beware of the voices of the world, especially when they are disguised in religious piety. They lead to emptiness and separation from God, and particularly from others. They are about building your kingdom, not God's kingdom.

3. The Challenge of the Nature of Our Neighbor

The truth be told, there are those who may not deserve our sensitivity, much less our sacrifice. Some are caught up in playing games. Some "neighbors" are manipulators, liars and deceivers. We hesitate to get too close lest we get caught up in their web. There are always those who take advantage, seek to possess, and love us and then leave us. Many well-intentioned believers have been scarred by past relationships and fear running the risk of loving a neighbor sacrificially.

However, in the face of all these realities, Christ commands us to reach out to others, to get involved in their messy lives, to love them unconditionally. He came and loved when it meant great sacrifice to self, when it required that He minister to a world that rarely would reach back and minister to Him—a world that would use Him, misunderstand Him, malign and even crucify Him; a fickle world that loved Him and then left Him. It is His powerful example that enables us to cut through the challenges of our pride and self-centeredness, the world without, and the way others so often behave.

Jonah's Failure to Love His Neighbor

The believer must be intentional to internalize his commitment to love his neighbor as an expression of his love for God. Jonah's lack of love for the Ninevites was essentially an expression of his lack of love for God. He is a strong example of how selfish pride and prejudice can seriously impair the work of God, and place in peril the lost souls dependent upon the servant chosen to deliver God's truth and love.

> The voice of the world will always tell you that life is about you. Beware the voices of the world, especially when they are disguised in religious piety.

As we look honestly at our own Christian lives, we can easily see how much of this "self" remains in each of us. It is so often "self" who attempts to live the Christian life—the mere fact that we use the word "try" so often indicates that it is "self" whom we make responsible. It is "self", too, who is often doing the Christian work. It is always "self" who gets irritable, envious, resentful, critical and worried. It is "self" who is hard and unyielding in its attitudes to others. It is" self" who is shy, self-conscious and reserved at the cost of reaching out to others. No wonder we, like Jonah, need breaking and discipline!

Jonah's reluctance to do God's will was a reflection of his deeply-rooted pride which always takes our emphasis off of others and places it on ourselves. As long as "self" is in control, God can accomplish very little with us that really matters, for the fruit of the Spirit (Galatians 5) with which God longs to fill us is the complete antithesis of the hard, unbroken spirit so often operating within us. The fruit of the Spirit presupposes that "self" has indeed been crucified. Therefore, being broken is both God's work and ours. He brings His pressure (His loving discipline) to bear, but we must make the choice to surrender.

If we are truly open to conviction as we seek fellowship with God, (and our willingness to submit to God is the prime condition of fellowship with Him) God will show us clearly the ugly expressions of our proud, hard "self" that causes Him the greatest pain. Then we can either stiffen our necks and refuse to repent, *or* we can bow our head and say, "Yes, Lord, I bow my heart to your will." Brokenness in daily experience is simply the response of a humble heart to the conviction of sin. And as the need for conviction is continuous in the life of the believer, we will likewise need to be broken continually.

PAUSE TO PONDER

Principles for Godly Living
Loving Others Through Serving

1. While preaching repentance is indeed fundamental, doing justice must be inseparably attached to it.
2. There are no incidental or accidental things in the life of the believer.
3. God is constantly working on multiple levels.
4. The truth of the spoken word accompanied by a transformed life is doubly profound and full of potential impact upon the lives of others.
5. People must know we care before we can be trusted with a platform to speak.
6. The challenge of pride within the heart will always be a voice pulling us in a direction toward self—never toward others.
7. The greatest paradox of all is that God takes the human heart with all its depravity and transforms it into something submissive, tender and beautiful.

Questions for Life Application

1. How has your understanding of loving God by serving others been awakened and deepened through Jonah's example? What new insights into Jesus' greatest commandment (to love God with all your heart and others as yourself) have you gained through the study of Jonah?

Story Three: A Recap

Perhaps the greatest paradox of all is that God takes the human heart with all its rebellion, deception, evil and selfishness and transforms it into something submissive, tender and beautiful—when and only when we cooperate with His process. This is the miracle of *true* repentance—not simply sorrow over sin, but truly seeing our sinful nature as an affront to a holy God and being willing to *turn away* from it.

How stubborn is the human heart! There are simply no adjectives strong enough to describe it! On the other hand, what kind of extravagant love is the Father's love! The words are equally difficult to come by. His grace is greater than our deepest sin—our pride , our arrogance, our false humility. How amazing that despite the rebellious nature of the creatures He made, God is still willing that no one perish and that all come to salvation and eternal life! What kind of love is this? As the great hymn states, it is "a love so amazing, so divine—(it surely) demands my soul, my life—my all."[1]

The biblical record leaves no doubt that Jonah did indeed deliver God's message of coming wrath. He did indeed follow through with his assignment—*but*—sadly he did it without a broken heart. He said the words God demanded him to say, but he lacked a heart of sensitivity, compassion and sacrifice that should have accompanied the words. The words were robotically spoken while the heart remained unmoved!

"In forty days, Nineveh *shall* be overthrown!"

The biblical record makes perfectly clear that Jonah's heart was still in desperate need of further humbling. Jonah accomplished the mission but it soon becomes evident that he found himself actually enjoying the preaching of God's wrath. He did it with abandon, not with tears, because his air of superiority continued operating fiercely within his heart. He couldn't wait for God's wrath to fall upon the Ninevites. His continuing story recorded in Jonah 4 makes this fact crystal clear.

> "But what God did was so terrible—to Jonah—that he burned with *anger* . . ." (Jonah 4:1)

What is most astounding is that the Most High God, nevertheless, responded to Nineveh's actions with unprecedented mercy.

> "When God examined their deeds, how they forsook their evil way, *He renounced the disaster* He had said He would do to them, and *He did not carry it out.*" (Jonah 3:10)

At this, Jonah was plunged back into his familiar emotional pit of despair and disappointment with God. The struggle was all too real, and Jonah was once more back to "Square 1." His response, after all he had suffered greatly and overcome, is utterly breathtaking, leaving us with a fresh reminder that like Jonah, our own engrained patterns of pride and old ways of thinking are *very* difficult to break. They are, as Paul describes them, *strongholds* that must be shattered if we are to be of any use to God. God's assessment of the human heart is proven accurate once more: indeed, we humans are a stiff-necked, stubborn, prideful lot!

Where would we be without the mercy of a loving God who forgives us and sets us on the path of His righteousness over and over again? Thanks be to the Most High God . . . His mercies are new every morning—*great is His faithfulness! In spite of man's rebellious nature, the Most High God is willing that no one perish but that all come to repentance (and eternal life).*

NOTE

1. Watts, Isaac. *When I Survey the Wondrous Cross.* 1707. Public domain.

Story 4

Running Into God

Jonah 4

Principle Truth:

Attempts at ministry are futile without love.

Key Concepts:

Doctrine:	The Blood of the Lamb
Attribute of God:	The Humility of Christ
Character Trait:	Loving Others through Sacrifice

Chapter 10

God Relents, Nineveh Repents and Jonah Resents!

Attempts at ministry are futile without love.

The people of Nineveh were acting strangely. Even the king abandoned his throne, threw down his royal robes, dressed himself in the heavy burlap of mourning, and sat down in the dirt. The inhabitants of the city were astounded at his "less than royal" behavior, but overwhelmingly and without exception, they too followed his example! The king went so far as to issue a sweeping public proclamation throughout the city authorized by his royal signet and with the full approval of his leaders. The power of a great awakening in Nineveh was on full display in his declaration:

> "Hear Ye! Hear Ye! Not one drop of water, not one bit of food shall touch the lips of man, woman or animal—including your herds and flocks! Dress them all in burlap, both people and animals, and send up a cry for help to the Most High God. Everyone must turn around . . . all of us must turn back from our evil lives and the violent actions that stain our hands. Who knows? Maybe the Most High God will be merciful to us; maybe

He will turn around and change His mind about us; maybe, just maybe, He will cease from His anger toward us and let us live!"

And indeed, God saw what they had done—that they were listening to Jonah's message and turning from their evil ways. And in great mercy and compassion, God changed His mind about them. What He said He would do to them, He did not do. To say that this was a stunning reversal of God's intention to destroy them would be an understatement!

The hymn writer, Frederick W. Faber, speaks of the infinite expanse of God's mercy stating: "There is a wideness in God's mercy—like the wideness of the sea . . . ." Yet, even the sea is not wide enough to describe this particular aspect of God's character, for the apostle Paul states in Ephesians 3:17–19:

> ". . . And may you, having been deeply rooted and securely grounded in love (mercy), be fully capable of comprehending with all the saints *the width and length and height and depth* of his love (mercy); and that you may come to know practically, through personal experience, the love (mercy) of Christ which *far surpasses mere knowledge*, that you may be filled up to all the fullness of God."

The mercy of the Most High God upon Nineveh was completely unexpected, but incredibly Jonah was furious that God relented. What irony! Having just preached to the most challenging audience of his life—with an overwhelmingly positive response down to the last person—why in heaven's name would Jonah have a meltdown of furious rage? He simply could not fathom God's actions and therefore, exploded in utter frustration!

> "God! I knew it! When I was back home long before all these horrible events happened to me, I knew it! That is why I ran off to Tarshish! I knew You were a God of sheer grace and mercy; I knew that You are not easily angered, and that You are rich in love and ready, at the drop of a hat, to turn Your plans of

punishment into a program of forgiveness! So, God, if You insist on refusing to judge them, you simply must kill me instead! I would be far better off dead than alive! It is agonizing to watch this wicked, godless, depraved city delivered from the destruction it so rightly deserves!"

Jonah had replaced the Most High God as his primary joy and the love of his life. He had lost his first love.

"But I have this against you, that you have left your first love. So remember the heights from which you have fallen and repent . . ." (Revelation 2:4–5)

The Most High God had been demoted. He no longer held first place in Jonah's heart. Yes, Jonah had a relationship with God, but there was obviously something else he valued more. His explosive anger revealed that he was willing to allow his relationship with God to be relegated to second place *if* he did not get this "thing" that was so vitally important to him. Essentially, he said to God,

"I will not serve you, God, if you do not give me _____."

This attitude of demanding that God conform to Jonah's requirements was a stunning revelation that something other than God Himself had taken over Jonah's heart. Jonah was, therefore, saying to God—who should have been the only real source of meaning in his life—

"I no longer have a purpose, God! If You refuse to relent in bringing your judgment upon Nineveh, just take my life! Kill me instead, for life is simply not worth living apart from seeing them face your well-deserved wrath!"

Just what usurped God's rightful place in Jonah's life? It had everything to do with the national interests of Jonah's homeland—his nation: the nation of Israel. Nineveh's repentance was pleasing to God—a sweet aroma to Him—but it threatened Israel's security. The nation of Assyria was Israel's most formidable enemy. The will of God for Nineveh and the political fortunes of Israel, in the mind of Jonah, were at odds with one another. It seemed logical that one would have to override the other, and Jonah left no doubt as to which of these two concerns was more important to him personally.

Make no mistake. Assyria was indeed a terrorist state, but Jonah refused to leave the matter in God's able hands. He refused to turn to God with his anxieties, his confusion and his doubts. He refused to trust God to do all things right and well. If he had to choose between the security of his beloved Israel and his loyalty to God, he was proving by his actions that God was to be pushed away, replaced. If love for one's country's interests leads to exploitation of people, or in Jonah's case, applauding for an entire class of people to remain spiritually lost, then love of that nation is more important than love of God, and *this* is by any definition, a form of idolatry.

As a missionary, Jonah should have been glad that the Ninevites had taken their first step toward his God—the Most High God. The people of the city had miraculously and overwhelmingly displayed a willingness to repent of their wicked way of life, and Jonah should have been eager to help them continue in their quest for truth by teaching them the character of this new God, and what it means to be in a covenant relationship with Him. On the contrary, Jonah was furious that they had taken that first step; that they had begun to move toward "his God."

It is most ironic that Jonah prayed earlier the following words from the belly of the fish: ". . . those who cling to idols *forfeit God's love* (mercy)" (Jonah 2:8). From his horrific experience in the sea, he recognized his own need for grace to a certain extent, but there was still much pride remaining, causing him (in his own words) to miss the grace of God—to be blind to it, to "forfeit" it. Pagans have idols—but not Jonah! Yes, of course he needed mercy and grace as we all do, but surely he wasn't on the same level as *these* people. Surely he still had some spiritual merit—surely he still had *some* claims on "his" God.

The social psychologist Jonathan Haidt concludes from his research that "self-righteousness is the normal human condition."[1] This statement concurs with what the Bible says about the inevitable human desire to justify oneself through performance and effort, and therefore to "boast" in one's own righteousness, race, pedigree or accomplishments (Jeremiah 9:23–26). Jonah's self-righteousness had been diminished somewhat through God's severe discipline, but obviously not destroyed. He cried out in his prayer from chapter 2, "Salvation comes only from the LORD!" Yet, he refused to let go of his false assumption: ". . . But I am not like those awful pagans!" *This is the very reason he was still susceptible to the spiritual crash that occurred in the final events of the book (after God showed Nineveh mercy).* He still stubbornly hung on to the notion that to some degree, God's mercy had to be deserved, and according to him, the Ninevites simply did not deserve it!

Rather than going back into the city and fulfilling his role as prophet and messenger of God (teaching the people deeper truth and preaching to them of God's love), Jonah stayed outside the city gates, in hopes that perhaps God would once again "relent in the opposite direction" and judge the city's inhabitants. But the Most High God spoke to Jonah saying,

"Jonah, what do *you* have to be angry about? Who are *you* to be angry with Me?"

Jonah, however, was so enraged that he refused to speak to God and instead turned away, strutted out of the city to the east, and sat down alone to sulk. He constructed a small makeshift shelter of leafy branches and sat in its shade pouting because of God's new word regarding the people of Nineveh. Jonah's pitiful reaction to the will of God for the lost was a powerful indication of the state of his heart! Remarkably, it still reeked of pride, and along with that, an ugly sense of entitlement.

After all he had been through—after all he had seen of the mighty hand of his God in delivering him from certain death and preserving his life—he was still in desperate need of a heart change. He simply refused to allow himself to love the people he had grown so accustomed to hating. He believed them to be too evil for God to show His favor toward them and furthermore, the Most High God was *his God—not theirs*! Yes, he had done as God had asked, but his obedience was conditional for he withdrew from further ministry, isolated himself, and built his little shelter where he could feel sorry for himself while continuing to question the mysterious workings of a God whose ways he refused to accept!

Jonah in his reluctant "obedience" was more pathetic than Jonah in his blatant disobedience! It is ironic, but entirely possible, to obey God but to do so with such a degree of reluctance that as far as God is concerned, the "obedience" is no better than the outright disobedience. It is always the state of the heart that matters to God.

Attempts at ministry are futile without love. Jonah did make the long journey to Nineveh, but refused to identify with the people to whom he had been sent. Something was dreadfully wrong. There is a powerful lesson in Jonah's reaction. Our own attitudes and actions, both good and evil, always reveal the state of our heart. Sharing mere words about God's love is nothing more than empty rhetoric apart from the heart being engaged in the sharing of the message. If even a root of pride remains, the message is compromised and far less effective than God intends it to be. Pride is deadly and robs us of the anointing of God upon our ministry.

> It is always the state of the heart that matters to God.

Jonah walked right through the city, preached a powerful evangelistic message, and departed as quickly as possible. He then proceeded to pout about the great success of his campaign. The problem in his heart is on display with unquestionable clarity! He felt in the very marrow of his bones, that his special love of God should not be extended to Gentiles, above all, to evil Gentiles like the inhabitants of Assyria. Throughout the entire narrative, Jonah grappled with this ongoing argument:

> "I just *knew* You might do something like this! They responded! All of them—from the king down to the animals! Everyone of them responded! But these people are *evil*! They only changed

because they were scared of You. They didn't actually convert and start worshipping You. They merely promised to start changing, and You are now showering Your mercy upon them for *that!* It's wonderful that you are a God of mercy, but this time, You have simply gone too far! Just how can You keep Your promises to uphold Your own people, and at the same time show this undeserved favor to Your peoples' cruelest enemies? How can You claim to be a God of justice, and yet allow their unspeakable evil and violence to go unpunished?"

Perhaps what is most tragic about Jonah's reluctance to accept God's mercy toward Nineveh and complete his mission is the fact that after Nineveh's unprecedented awakening, eventually the Assyrian capital city was indeed destroyed, and the destruction of that city was used by Jesus centuries later as an example of the worst judgment that ever happened to any city up to that time in history (Matthew 12:41; Luke 11:30,32).

Could it be that the awakening of the Ninevites did not lead to genuine repentance and conversion because God's chosen messenger to them refused to identify with these lost people? Instead of making sacrifices for them by living among them, loving them, building them up, teaching and equipping them, and grounding them in God's ways, His truth, and His righteousness, Jonah simply—half-heartedly—delivered the message, sat in his little booth and complained:

"The Most High God is *my* God—He doesn't belong to these despicable people! They are barbarians! He belongs to *me*! I don't like these people. I don't like the way they look, the way they dress, the way they smell, their habits, and I despise their customs. They don't understand my Jewish ways; therefore, I refuse to be among them. I will just sit in my little booth all by myself and isolate myself! I did what I was sent here to do, but I will do nothing more!"

So Jonah launched his little separatist movement in which he established his own independent "church"—The First Church of *Me, Myself and I!* He did this all because he hated his assignment and refused to move on with Step Two in Nineveh's awakening to righteousness. He refused to become the human role model of his message by loving the people from his heart. He had not budged in nursing his hatred of these people. He still loved hating the very ones he had been sent to save. His prideful attitude would eventually produce deadly results for the Ninevites—results that were entirely dependent upon his choice of obedience or disobedience to this mission. *Attempts at ministry are futile without love.*

GOING DEEPER

DOCTRINE: THE BLOOD OF THE LAMB

The Problem is in Us!

Perhaps the book of Jonah is so appealing to readers throughout the centuries because we can relate so well to the main character. Pride is the driving force in the life of Jonah, and it operates in the same manner in our lives as well. It is an incredibly strong force of evil that is often undetectable until circumstances bring it into the light. It loves to hide and masquerade in the form of false humility. Pride drives us to establish, protect, enhance and maintain our own sense of worth. It serves to guard and promote our significance at all costs. Pride causes us to never say we are sorry. It forces us to take the credit, to belittle others, and to compete with the significance of others. It makes us seek higher and better places, establish social credentials, and claim our rights and privileges even to the detriment of those around us. Pride seeks to keep us on top and leads us on relentless searches for even higher platforms in order to display our significance.

If left to itself, pride will dominate every thought, every situation, every relationship and every conversation. Clearly, it is a major detriment to an intimate and growing relationship with God. We learn from

Proverbs 6:16–17 that pride is first on the list of things that are "detest-able" to God. Anything that creates such hostility in the heart of God is a serious matter. Peter confirmed God's hostility to the proud as he states:

"Likewise, you younger men, be subject to your elders; and all of you, clothe yourselves with humility toward one another, for God is opposed to the proud, but He gives grace to the humble. Therefore, humble yourselves under the mighty hand of God so that He may exalt you." (1 Peter 5:5–6)

Pride also compels us to elevate ourselves above God and declare ourselves to become the god of our lives. "I'll call the shots and deter-mine my own destiny" is the motto of the proud. We must keep in mind the sobering warning that pride precedes a fall (Proverbs 16:18). Pride makes the arrogant claim that: "I am more important than the God of the universe and the God who created me!" It is an individual's "in-your-face" declaration to God. Every time I do what I want to do and ignore what God requires me to do, I am elevating my own importance over His Lordship. Every time I ignore God's word, His will and His way, I am saying that something else is more important to me than God. Jonah is the perfect example of this deadly character flaw, and we are wise to examine God's remedy to counter it.

The Solution is in Christ's Blood

There is only one thing in the world that can cleanse us from our pride (the underlying cause of *all* sin) and give us freedom and victory. *The power of the blood of the Lord Jesus Christ is the only remedy to defeat pride.* We must understand what it is that gives the blood of Christ its mighty power with God on behalf of men, for only then, will we under-stand the conditions upon which its full power can be experienced in our personal lives. The blessings ascribed to man through the blood of Christ are overwhelming and numerous. Appropriating these blessings leads to a life of meaning, purpose, peace, power, and the intimate presence of and communion with the Most High God. For a deeper understanding of these blessings, the reader should meditate upon Hebrews 9 and 10. Just a few of the benefits to the believer are listed below:

1. Peace.

By His blood, peace is made between man and God.

2. Forgiveness.

By His blood, there is forgiveness of sins and eternal life for all who put their faith in the Lord Jesus.

3. Power.

By His blood, the power of Satan is overcome.

4. Cleansing.

By His blood, there is power for continual cleansing from all sin for us.

5. Deliverance.

By His blood, we are set free from the tyranny of an evil conscience to serve the living God.

6. Presence of God.

By His blood, the most unworthy have liberty to enter the Holy of Holies of God's presence.

"Therefore, believers, since we have confidence and full freedom to enter the Holy Place (the place where God dwells) by means of the blood of Jesus, by this new and living way which He initiated and opened for us through the veil that is, through His flesh and since we have a great and wonderful Priest who rules over the house of God . . . Let us approach God with a true and sincere heart in unqualified assurance of faith, having had our hearts sprinkled clean from an evil conscience and our bodies washed with pure water. Let us seize and hold tightly the confession of our hope without wavering, for He who promised is reliable and trustworthy and faithful to his word." (Hebrews 10:19–23)

What Gives the Blood its Power?

It is tragic but true: too often that precious blood does not have its cleansing, peace-giving, life-giving, sin-destroying power in the heart of the believer, and too often we do not find ourselves in God's presence enjoying fellowship with Him. What is missing when we do not or cannot live in victory over our struggles, and in Jonah's case, gain victory over his pride? The key is found in Revelation 12:11: "And they overcame *and* conquered him (Satan) because of the *blood of the Lamb* and because of the word of their testimony . . . ." It is not the blood of "the Warrior," but the blood of "the Lamb" that John mentions in his account found in the book of Revelation! That which gives the blood its power with God for men, therefore, is ironically the lamb-like disposition of the One who shed that blood as the supreme expression of surrender to the Father's will.

The title "the Lamb" so frequently given to the Lord Jesus in Scripture is, first of all, a description of His finished work—being a sacrifice and a substitute by standing in our place for our sin. In Jonah's day, when a sinning Israelite wanted to get right with God, it was the blood of an innocent lamb (sometimes a goat) which had to be shed and whose blood was sprinkled on the altar. Jesus is the divine fulfillment of all those sacrificial lambs that men offered throughout the Old Testament times—He is *the* Lamb of God who takes away the sin of the world. But the title "the Lamb" has deeper meaning still. It describes Christ's character. He is the Lamb in that He is meek and lowly in heart, gentle and unresisting, and all the time surrendering His own will to the Father's will, for the blessing and saving of men and women like you and me.

Anyone but the Lamb would have resented and resisted the treatment men inflicted upon Him. But He, in obedience to the Father and out of love for us, did neither. Men did what they wanted to Him, and for our sakes, He yielded every time without fail. When He was reviled, He reviled not. When He suffered, He threatened not. No standing up for His rights, no hitting back, no resentment, no complaining!

How different is His disposition from ours! When the Father's will and the malice of men joined forces pointing to Calvary, Jesus, the Lamb of God, bowed His head in willingness and submission for that as well. It was as the Lamb that Isaiah saw Christ when he prophesied, "He is brought as a lamb to the slaughter, and as a sheep before her shearers is dumb, so He opened not His mouth." The scourging, the spitting, the hair plucked from his cheeks, the last march up Calvary's hill to the cross, the nails, the lifting up, the piercing of His side and the flowing of His blood—none of these things would ever have been, had He not been the Lamb. And all this to pay the price of *my* sin, *your* sin!

> Anyone but the Lamb would have resented and resisted the treatment men inflicted upon Him.

Every mention of the blood should call to mind the deep humility and self-sacrifice of the Lamb, for *it was this very disposition that gives the blood its wonderful power with God.* "How much more shall the blood of Christ, who through the eternal Spirit offered Himself without spot to God . . ." (Hebrews 9:14). And it is this fact as well that imparts the power with God for the believer. *This is the disposition that is of supreme value to God. This is the disposition He honors.* Humility and the surrender of one's will to God are the attitudes He looks for from His children—those who call themselves followers of Jesus.

Like the Master, so shall the servant be. In fact, it was to manifest all this that God created the first man. It was Adam's refusal to walk this very path of surrender that constituted his first sin—and it has been the heart of sinful attitudes and actions ever since. It was to bring this lamb-like disposition back to earth that Jesus came and demonstrated it so beautifully for us. It was simply because the Father saw this in the Son that He could say, "My Son, in whom I am well pleased." It was because the shedding of His blood so supremely expressed this disposition that it is so utterly precious to God and vital for us to understand and appropriate.

Experiencing the Blood's Full Power in Our Lives

Only a willingness to possess the same disposition that ruled Christ, and by bending our necks in brokenness as He bowed His, can we experience the full power of the blood of the Lamb. Just as it is the disposition of the Lamb that gives the blood its power, so it is only as we are willing to be partakers of this same disposition of the Lamb that we will know its full power in our lives as well. The good news is that *we can be partakers of Christ's disposition* because it has been made transferable to us by His death. All the fruits of the Spirit listed in Galatians 5—love, joy, peace, longsuffering, gentleness, goodness, faith, meekness, self-control—what are these but the expressions of the Lamb-like nature of Jesus Christ with which the Holy Spirit seeks to fill us! Jesus—though exalted now to the throne of God—is still the Lamb of God, and He is passionate about reproducing Himself and these godly attributes in *you!*

The Problem of Resistance

Make no mistake! There is indeed a hard, unyielding self, which stands up only for itself and resists the way of righteousness. This must be broken if we are to ever assume the disposition of the Lamb and if the precious blood is to reach us in its full cleansing power. Every sin we commit is the result of this hard, unbroken self taking up some attitude of pride in us, and we will not find peace through the blood until we are willing to see the source of each sin and reverse the wrong attitude that caused it through our *specific* naming of it and repentance of it—always a humbling experience!

Walking in the light exposes any sin that may be present, and the light brings a special spiritual sensitivity to realize that the Lord is prodding us to action—to perform all kinds of costly acts of repentance and surrender, even those "small" things we may consider trivialities. Their importance can be gauged by what it costs our pride to make them right. It may be a confession or an apology to someone that is needful. It may be an act of restitution or a yielding of our own rights in a certain situation. It may be to go to the one who has wronged you and confess to him the far greater wrong of your resentment toward him. We may be called to be open and transparent with a friend that he may know us as we really are, so that we may finally enjoy true fellowship together. These "reparations" may well be humiliating and a complete reversal of our usual attitudes of pride, superiority and selfishness; however, by acting in humility, we will experience true brokenness and actually become a partaker in the humility of Christ.

> The only beautiful thing about the Christian is Jesus Christ!

As we exercise humility and a willingness to submit in each issue God brings to light, the blood of the Lamb will cleanse us from all sin and enable us to walk with God as white as snow with perfect peace in our hearts along with the sweet intimacy of His presence. The simple truth is this: the only beautiful thing about the Christian is Jesus Christ! Oh! For more of Him!

PAUSE TO PONDER

Principles for Godly Living
The Blood of the Lamb

1. It is possible to obey God but to do so with such a degree of reluctance that as far as God is concerned, our "obedience" is no better than outright disobedience.
2. Our attitudes and actions, both good and evil, always reveal the state of the heart.
3. The heart must be engaged in sharing God's message; otherwise, the message is empty rhetoric.
4. Pride is deadly and robs us of the anointing of God.
5. Our lives must be the human role model of our message.
6. Every time I do what I want to do and ignore what God requires me to do, I elevate my own importance over His Lordship.

7. The power of the blood of the Lord Jesus Christ is the only remedy to defeat pride.

8. Only through our willingness to possess the same disposition that ruled Christ can we experience the full power of His blood.

Questions for Life Transformation

1. How are pride and self-sufficiency bearing bad fruit that nevertheless, might look good on the outside in your life? What do you think God may be bringing to life in you in exposing these deadly attitudes?

2. What do anger, frustration and negativity reflect about the state of your heart? What connection do you see between these attitudes and "clinging to idols and forfeiting God's grace"?

3. Why is the condition of "self-righteousness" so difficult to see when evaluating oneself? Will you commit to an accountability partner who will help expose this deadly attitude in you? Name your partner and ask for their help.

4. How has studying the life of Jonah deepened your understanding of the power of Jesus' blood shed for you? What does this precious blood mean to you personally?

NOTE

1. Haidt, Jonathan. "The Age of Outrage: What the Current Political Climate is Doing to Our Country and Our Universities." *City Journal*, Dec. 17, 2017, https://www.city-journal.org/html/age-outrage-15608.html. Accessed 27 February 2020.

Jonah's Anger Prompts
God's Questions

Attempts at ministry are futile without love.

The discipline of God dramatically intersected Jonah's life through the deadly storm recorded in chapter one, and he survived only because of the mercy of God. He too, like Nineveh, deserved only judgment but nevertheless, received God's mercy, and was glad for it. Now in the midst of the godless people of Assyria, all prior events—as astounding as they were—had become dull and virtually forgotten. Jonah had hardened his heart once again and become the ungrateful servant of Jesus' New Testament parable. Having been forgiven himself, he refused to forgive others (Matthew 18:21–35). God, however, was not yet finished with His prophet, and would thus orchestrate the remaining events of this account in order to bring Jonah to a fresh understanding of the aspect of God's character with which he continued to struggle—the mercy of a loving God toward all people!

Every time it seemed that Jonah was given a firsthand demonstration of God's grace, it turned out that he still had further to go to reach the bedrock of his own sinful heart. Until that place was reached, permanent change could not be accomplished. As long as there is something more important than God in the heart, one will be, like Jonah, fragile, judgmental and self-righteous. Whatever *it* is, *it* will create pride and an inclination to look down upon those who do not have *it*. It will also create fear, anxiety and insecurity. *It* is the basis for your happiness, and if anything threatens *it*, you will be overwhelmed with anger and despair.

> "To reach the bedrock of God's grace in the deepest recesses of the heart is to recognize all the ways we make good things into idols and ways of saving ourselves."[1]

We must finally come to the place where we recognize that we all—no exceptions—live wholly by God's grace. In fact, every breath we take is evidence of God's grace sustaining our lives. The understanding of grace enables us to serve the Lord, not in order to get things from Him but just for *Him*, for His own sake, just for who He is, for the joy of knowing Him, delighting in Him, and becoming like Him. When the bedrock of the heart is finally reached, God's grace can do its work of draining us, slowly but surely, of our self-righteousness and fear.

> Every breath we take is evidence of God's grace sustaining our lives.

God chose to accomplish the final disciplinary episode of Jonah's life in a powerfully probing manner. There was no sermon, no rebuke, no argument—just a barbed question that must have hung like a fish hook in the bedrock of Jonah's heart. Almighty God simply asked His servant a loaded question,

"Jonah, *have you any right* to be angry?"

Questions! God asked Jonah a simple question. Asking questions is one of God's most creative ways of correcting us and placing His finger on the issue that is troubling us. He frequently uses questions to help us discover the eternal issues of life. There are numerous examples throughout the Scriptures from Genesis to Revelation:

"Adam, *where are you?*"

"Cain, *where is your brother?*"

"Saul, *what is this bleating of the sheep I hear?*"

"Isaiah, *who will go for us?*"

"Jonah, *have you any right to be angry? What do you have to be angry about?*"

The question God asked Jonah struck a sensitive chord as God used His inquiry to "call Jonah out!" God's question angered the prophet all the more. His pride and stubborn prejudice caused him to falsely believe he knew better than God! God, however, was gentle in asking this simple question, for His intention was to show Jonah that it is entirely possible to have the right theology but still possess a heart full of pride. There was something deadly wrong still. Jonah's pharisaical superiority broke the heart of God, robbing Jonah of the peace and joy of a job well done. Jonah left no room for God's pleasure or encouragement. There was no commendation with words every believer longs to hear . . .

> "Jonah, you have done a wonderful job with your assignment! Just look at your success! All Nineveh was awakened through your mighty preaching! You were tremendous! So . . . let's just forget about your anger, your prejudice and your pride, and just pretend they aren't here . . . "

No! No! A thousand times no! God refused to ignore Jonah's deepest flaw. He put His finger directly on the thing that mattered most, even more than Nineveh's corporate repentance at that moment in time, and thus, said to Jonah,

> It is entirely possible to have the right theology but still possess a heart full of pride.

> "Jonah, there is anger inside you still, and you *must* deal with it. It will destroy you if you continue to refuse to address it. What right have you to be angry? Who are

you to presume to understand My mysterious ways? You have no idea of the love in my heart for these people!"

There were no answers to these questions. The questions simply indicated the need for further discipline. One final lesson was yet needful.

Wasting no time, God arranged for a broad-leafed tree to spring up. It grew up in a single day and covered Jonah, cooling him off from the sweltering heat of the sun and abruptly altering his ugly state of sulking to a more pleasant state of temporary contentment. Jonah was pleased at this new development, and for a brief moment enjoyed the comforting shade of this unexpected plant that had appeared seemingly out of nowhere.

However, just when it seemed that life was beginning to improve, God sent an inconvenience—an irritation. A worm appeared, and by dawn of the next day, the worm had bored into the shade tree causing it to wither away completely and die. The shade gradually fell away allowing the scorching sun to rise yet again to meet the new day, and along with the blistering heat, God sent a hot, blinding wind that rose up mercilessly from the east. The sun beat down relentlessly upon Jonah's head, and he started to faint. Once again, Jonah's familiar "companion" called "Misery" came rushing in as his thoughts turned to the unfathomable ways of a God he knew he would never fully comprehend. He, then, prayed to die.

"Oh, God, I am far better off dead than in all this misery! I hate this place, I hate these people, I hate my life. I just want to die!"

But once more, God asked an additional question attempting finally to reach the bedrock of Jonah's deeply-rooted heart issues,

"What right do you have to get angry about this shade tree and the worm and the wind?"

And Jonah said to God,

"Plenty of right! Everything that has happened to me and is happening to me now—all this—has made me angry enough to die!"

But God replied to Jonah,

"What is this nonsense? How is it that you can change your feelings from pleasure to anger overnight about a mere shade tree that you did absolutely nothing to get? Where did it come from, Jonah? You neither planted nor watered it. It grew up out of nowhere in one night and died the next night. So, why can't I, likewise, change what I feel about Nineveh from anger to pleasure in the course of one day, this big city of more than 120,000 childlike people who don't yet know right from wrong, to say nothing of all the innocent animals?

The word used in verses 10–11 for "compassion" is a word that means to grieve over someone or something, to have your heart broken, to weep for it. In light of God's great compassion, essentially He was saying to Jonah,

"You had compassion for the plant—you wept over it, Jonah. Your heart became attached to it. When it died, it grieved you. What a revelation! You weep over plants, *but my compassion is for people!*" What happens in Nineveh affects Me! It moves Me! It grieves Me! And you have yet to really grasp this!"

Attempts at ministry are futile without love.

Note: Commentators have identified the plant that grew up over night as the Ricinus or castor oil plant, which grows very quickly and provides shade with its broad leaves.[2]

GOING DEEPER

ATTRIBUTE OF GOD: THE HUMILITY OF CHRIST

The Greatest Enemy of Humility

The late John R. W. Stott, a remarkably humble man of great abilities and accomplishments who is often credited for making the greatest impact for Christ in the twentieth century, said: "Pride is man's greatest enemy, while humility is our greatest friend."[3] Tragically few of us realize just how dangerous and deadly pride is to the soul, and how greatly it hinders our intimacy with God and our love for others. Humility, on the other hand, is often viewed as weakness, and few of us know much about it or intentionally pursue it. Nevertheless, for the sake of our soul and our potential impact for Christ, we are wise to acquire a clearer understanding of pride and humility, and how to forsake the one to embrace the other.

> "The essential vice, the utmost evil is pride. Impurity, anger, greed, drunkenness, and all that, are mere flea bites in comparison: it was through Pride that the devil became the devil; Pride leads to every other vice: It is the complete anti-God state of mind . . . It is Pride which has been the chief cause of misery in every nation and every family since the world began. It is the devil's most effective and destructive tool."[4]

The Outworkings of Pride

It is easy to see the outworking of pride in the affairs of individuals, families, nations and cultures. Romans 1 paints a sobering picture of its devastating path. As people lose or suppress the knowledge of God, spiritual darkness grows and a psychological inversion occurs: in their prideful thinking, God becomes smaller and they become larger. The center of gravity in their mental lives shifts from God to themselves. They become the center of their world, and God is conveniently moved to the periphery, either through denial of His existence or distortion of His character. Self-importance and godless self-confidence grow stronger.

The cycle that follows is familiar: people exalt themselves against God and over others. Pride increases, arrogant and abusive behavior ensues, and people suffer the outpouring of the wrath of God. The apostle Paul gives a clear and unquestionable depiction of the downward progression:

> "For the wrath of God is being revealed from heaven against

all the godlessness and wickedness of people, who suppress the truth by their wickedness. Since what may be known about God is plain to them, because God has made it plain to them. For since the creation of the world, God's invisible qualities—His eternal power and divine nature have been clearly seen, being understood from what has been made, so that people are without excuse.

For although they knew God, they neither glorified him as God nor gave thanks to him, but their thinking became futile and their foolish hearts were darkened. Although they claimed to be wise, they became fools and exchanged the glory of the immortal God for images made to look like a mortal human being and birds and animals and reptiles.

Therefore God gave them over in the sinful desires of their hearts to sexual impurity for the degrading of their bodies with one another. They exchanged the truth about God for a lie, and worshipped and served created things rather than the Creator—who is forever praised. Amen.

Because of this, *God gave them over* to shameful lusts. Even their women exchanged natural sexual relations for unnatural ones. In the same way the men also abandoned natural relations with women and were inflamed with lust for one another. Men committed shameful acts with other men, and received in themselves the due penalty for their error.

Furthermore, just as they did not think it worthwhile to retain the knowledge of God, so *God gave them over* to a depraved mind, so that they do what ought not to be done. They have become filled with every kind of wickedness, evil, greed and depravity. They are full of envy, murder, strife, deceit, and malice. They are gossips, slanderers, God-haters, insolent, arrogant and boastful; they invent ways of doing evil; they disobey their parents; they have no understanding, no fidelity, no love, no mercy. Although they knew God's righteous decree that those who do such things deserve death, they not only continue to do these very things but also approve of those who practice them." (Romans 1:18–31)

Pride's Most Subtle Form

Few people today seem to be aware of the danger of *spiritual pride* for it is often subtly disguised as righteousness. Jonathan Edwards rightly states: "Spiritual pride is the main door by which the devil comes into the hearts of those who are zealous about advancing the cause of Christ. It is the chief inlet of smoke from the bottomless pit darkening the mind and misleading the path. Pride is the chief source of all the mischief the Devil introduces to clog and hinder a work of God. Until this disease is cured, medicines are applied in vain to heal all other diseases."[5]

Pride takes many shapes and forms and affects all of us to some degree. The widespread, chronic preoccupation with the self, especially in American culture, is rooted in pride and gives rise to countless emotional problems. Pride is an attitude of self-sufficiency, self-importance and self-exaltation in relation to God. Toward others, it is an attitude of superiority, contempt and indifference. Pride is a spiritual cancer that eats up the very possibility of love, contentment or even common sense.

Pride provokes God's displeasure, and He has committed Himself to oppose it. If your pride causes you to exalt yourself, you are painting a target on your back and inviting God to open fire upon you! And He will. For He has declared His determination to bring your pride low wherever He finds it, whether among angels or humans, believers or unbelievers. Pride will be our undoing if we tolerate it in our lives.

The Blinding Power of Pride

Chances are very good that most of us do not see pride in our own lives. While it is quite easy to see it in others, it is very difficult to see it in ourselves. However, it is ironic that the more we have it in ourselves, the more we dislike it in others. It is critical that we identify its presence. The following are ways of detecting it:

- There is no more certain proof of the presence of pride than a belief that one is sufficiently humble.

- To determine if pride is a problem, just ask yourself: How much do I dislike it when people snub me, or refuse to take any notice of me? How incensed am I when another gains power or prestige that should belong to me (in my "humble" opinion!)?

- To identify if pride is present, ask God in prayer to reveal it in its most subtle forms—gossip, a critical spirit, jealousy, envy, an enjoyment of someone's misfortune. When pride is identified, confess it, repent of it and forsake it.

- To identify if pride is present, ask others—those who know you best—if they see any expressions of sinful pride or arrogance in your life. Ask someone close to you to be your accountability partner to identify the deadly presence of pride in you.

When we exalt ourselves through pride, God does not seek to punish us and bring us low but rather forgive and restore us. He says again and again in Scripture, "humble yourselves and I will exalt you." This gives great hope and encouragement, for God takes pleasure in our efforts to humble ourselves, and He loves to bless and exalt the humble. For just as pride is the root of all sin, so humility is the root of all virtue.[6]

Humility: One of the Most Essential Characteristics of The Christian

Our perspective on humility is radically changed when we allow ourselves to meditate on the greatest example in all of history: the humility of our Lord Jesus Christ. By the very act of leaving heaven, coming to earth, and taking the form of man, He demonstrated an incredible humbling of Himself. He came "not to be served, but to serve, and to give His life a ransom for many" (Matthew 20:28). He asked His followers to model His example of servanthood by washing their dirty feet (John 13:1–11). Christ is the humility of God embodied in human nature. The apostle Paul urged the believers in Philippi:

> "Have this mind among yourselves which is yours in Christ Jesus, who, though He was in the form of God, did not count equality with God a thing to be grasped, but made Himself nothing, taking the form of a servant, being born in the likeness of men. And being found in human form, He humbled himself by becoming obedient to the point of death, even death on a cross." (Philippians 2:5–8)

The Dove and the Lamb: The Secret of Humility

Living in victory over pride and making impact for Christ are not the product of bettering ourselves and our hard work, but are simply the *fruit* of the power and presence of the Holy Spirit. We are not called upon to produce the fruit, but simply to bear the fruit. It is all the time to be *His fruit*. This is beautifully illustrated in the manner by which the Holy Spirit came upon Jesus at His baptism.

John the Baptist saw Jesus coming to him and said of Him, "Behold, the Lamb of God, which takes away the sin of the world." Then as John baptized Jesus, he saw the heavens open and the Spirit of God descending like a dove lighting upon Him. In his powerful book entitled *The Calvary Road*, Roy Hession describes the beauty of two powerful metaphors. There are two images depicted in the baptism of Christ that contain incredible meaning: the dove and the lamb—the dove descending upon the Lamb, resting herself upon Him! The lamb and the dove are surely the gentlest of all God's creatures. The lamb speaks of meekness and submission, and the dove of peace.[7] This shows clearly that the heart of our Lord Jesus is humility.

When God chose to reveal Himself in His Son, He gave Him the name of the "Lamb." And when it was necessary for the Holy Spirit to come into the world, He was revealed through the sign of the dove. The main lesson here is that the Holy Spirit, as the dove, could only come upon and remain upon the Lord Jesus because he was the Lamb. Had Jesus possessed any other disposition than that of the Lamb—humility, submissiveness and self-surrender, the dove could never have rested upon Him. Being herself so gentle, she would have been frightened away had not Jesus been meek and lowly in heart.

This is a poignant picture of the condition upon which the same Holy Spirit can come upon us and abide in us. The Dove (Holy Spirit) can only abide in us as we are willing to be as the Lamb (Jesus Christ). How impossible that He could rest upon us when "self" remains unbroken and "in charge!" The manifestations of the unbroken self are the direct opposite of the gentleness of the dove. Galatians 5 lists the nine attributes of the fruit of the Holy Spirit with which the Dove longs to fill the believer! The Spirit's fruit are contrasted with the ugly works of the flesh—the unbroken self that are listed as well in the same chapter. It is a stark contrast of a Wolf (in Sheep's clothing) with the gentle Dove.

The Disposition of the Lamb[8]

It is clear that the Holy Spirit will only come upon us and remain upon us as we too are willing to be as the Lamb in every area where He convicts us. As Jesus made His way to Calvary, we see the disposition that we too must be willing to possess and display, for like the Master, the servant must be. There are five "positions" of humility Christ assumed that must become ours as His followers:

1. He was the Simple Lamb.
A lamb is the simplest of God's creatures. It has no schemes or plans for helping itself—it exists in helplessness and simplicity. Jesus made Himself as nothing for us and became the simple Lamb. He had no strength of His own, or wisdom of His own; no

schemes to get Himself out of difficulties, just simple dependence on the Father all the time. We must be willing to be *simple* lambs.

2. He was the Shorn Lamb.

Jesus was willing to be shorn of His rights, His reputation, and every human liberty that was due Him, just as a lamb is shorn of its wool. He never resisted, for a lamb never does. When He was reviled for our sakes, He reviled not. When He suffered, He threatened not. He never said: "Don't treat Me like that! Don't you know that I am the Son of God!" But on so many occasions, we are unwilling to be shorn of what we consider to be our rights. The Dove must take His flight from us when we are unwilling to be shorn lambs.

3. He was the Silent Lamb.

"As a sheep before her shearers is dumb, so He opened not his mouth." We read that "He answered nothing." He never defended Himself, nor explained Himself. But we are anything but silent when others say unkind or untrue things about us. Our self-defense and self-vindication are so often on grand display to the world! We insist on defending ourselves and our rights! We excuse ourselves and rationalize our hurts when we should quickly admit our wrong. On every such occasion, the Dove must take His flight and withdraw His peace and blessing from our hearts—simply because we are not willing to be the *silent* Lamb.

4. He was the Spotless Lamb.

Not only did nothing escape His lips, but there was nothing in His heart except love for those who sent Him to the cross. There was no resentment, no grudge, no bitterness. Even as the nails were put through His hands and feet, He said, "I forgive you" and asked His Father to forgive them as well. But what resentment and bitterness resides in our hearts—toward this one or that one? The Dove is forced to fly away because we are not willing to bear the offense and forgive for Jesus' sake.

5. He was the Substitute Lamb.

The humility of the Lord Jesus in becoming our Lamb was necessary only that He might become on the cross our Substitute, our Scapegoat, carrying our sins in His own body so that there might be forgiveness of our sins and cleansing from all their stains when we repent of them. How devastating it is to see our sins wounding and hurting our Lord and others. May this solemn thought of "the Lamb of God" break our proud hearts in humble repentance, for it is only when we see these sins of ours and are broken and willing to repent of them, and make things right, that the powerful blood of the Lamb can cleanse us from them and the Dove can return with peace and bring His abundant blessing to our hearts.

Jonah's Resistance

Although Jonah lived in Old Testament times before Pentecost and God's gift of the indwelling Holy Spirit, the Spirit was nevertheless powerfully at work in the lives of God's messengers. As the prophets of God accepted their respective callings, God's Spirit moved mightily upon them as His will and mission was carried out in various ways. Because of Jonah's resistance to God's calling, however, the anointing of God's Holy Spirit upon the mission to Nineveh was compromised. Oh, that we might understand the relationship between the power of God upon us and the purity of an obedient heart fully submissive and humble before God.

Principles for Godly Living
The Humility of Christ

1. The only beautiful thing about the Christian is Jesus Christ!
2. To reach the bedrock of God's grace in the deepest recesses of the heart is to recognize all the ways we make good things into idols and ways of saving ourselves.
3. It is entirely possible to have the right theology but still possess a heart full of pride.
4. Few of us realize how dangerous pride is to the soul and how greatly it hinders our intimacy with God and our ability to love others.
5. Spiritual pride is the main door by which the devil comes into the hearts of those who are passionate about advancing the cause of Christ.
6. Pride is an attitude of self-sufficiency, self-importance and self-exaltation in relation to God.
7. Pride provokes God's displeasure, and He has committed Himself to oppose it.
8. While it is quiet easy to see pride in others, it is very difficult to see it in ourselves—the more we have it, the more we dislike it in others.

Questions for Life Transformation

1. How do you find balance between the tension of seeing yourself as "nothing" while still recognizing your standing as a child of God, deeply loved and valued by Him?
2. Have you made a "good thing" into an idol in your life? Confess and repent of this sin. Ask God to deepen your genuine love for Him alone.
3. Share your insights into God's questions of Jonah. Why is the asking of questions a powerful way to get to the root of a sin problem?
4. How is Satan using pride in *your* life today? Identifying this is the first step toward healing. Confess and repent!

NOTES

1. Keller, Timothy. *The Prodigal Prophet: Jonah and the Mystery of God's Mercy*. New York, Viking, 2018.

2. "Kikayon." *Wikipedia*, 11 January 2020, https://en.wikipedia.org/w/index.php?title=Kikayon&oldid=935177809. Accessed 18 February 2020.

3. Stott, John R. W. "The Living God is a Missionary God." *Perspectives on the World Christian Movement*. 4th ed. Pasadena, William Carey Library, 2009.

4. Lewis, C.S. *Mere Christianity*. Harper One, 2015.

5. Edwards, Jonathan. "Undetected Spiritual Pride: One Cause of Failure in Times of Great Revival." *Harmony Missionary Baptist Church*, http://grace-abounding.com/Articles/Sin/Pride_Edwards.htm. Accessed 27 February 2020.

6. John Chrysostom qtd. in Tarrants, Thomas A, III. "Pride and Humility." *Knowing & Doing: A Teaching Quarterly for Discipleship of Heart and Mind*, Winter 2011, http://www.cslewisinstitute.org/Pride_and_Humility_SinglePage. Accessed 3 March 2020.

7. Hession, Roy. *The Calvary Road: The Way of Personal Revival*. Winslow, Buckingham, Rickfords Hill Publishing Ltd., 1950.

8. The description of the Lamb is taken from an address given by Marshal Shallis, Secretary of the Evangelistic Society of London, England, titled "The Lamb and the Dove" which he adapted from the book, *The Calvary Road* by Roy Hession.

Chapter 12

God Expresses His Compassion For All People

Attempts at ministry are futile without love.

Through a series of powerful questions, Jonah was gently taken by the hand and allowed to see himself as he really was. He saw the fatal flaw of his pride standing like a giant boulder blocking the impact of what he was attempting to accomplish for his God! He saw that the whole of his life had been a self-centered, prideful mess. He saw that all he really cared about were lesser things—including himself, his desires, his passions, the wind, the worm and the weeds —that's all, just trivial things! He didn't really care about others at all, certainly not the people of Nineveh, and yet His calling was to be a missionary, to love people—lost people, the people of Assyria, Israel's greatest enemy! *Perhaps the greatest gift God can ever give a human being is to finally see oneself for what he really is—to see oneself as God sees him.*

Jonah realized he had become so angry at the worm and so angry about the vine because it withered, that nothing else really mattered, not even the 120,000 "little children" (lost and without hope) who were soon to perish if he failed to love them as he should. Essentially God was saying to Jonah,

"Jonah, you and I are looking at an identical situation in two totally different ways. I am pleased with what has happened here, and you are angry about it. *Now here's a question for you: which of us has the proper perspective?* My thoughts are not your thoughts, and whatever your thoughts and feelings may be, it is *always My assessment* that is the correct assessment—*not yours.*"

As Romans 3:4 states: "Let God be true and every man a liar!" In mercy, God challenged Jonah to reorder his perspective, for He loved this reluctant servant enough to correct him. Jonah had a warped view of things caused by pride and superiority. Only a radical transformation could produce genuine love for people he had so long hated. *Attempts at ministry are futile without love.* Once more, God reiterated His unwavering position. He expressed to Jonah exactly how He felt about people.

"Jonah, I love people; I love *all* people—the tall and the small, the wicked and the not so wicked, and I love the little ones—I love them all. I love every inhabitant in the city of Nineveh—all 120,000 of them. *They all matter to Me.* I love them all just as I love you."

GOING DEEPER

CHARACTER TRAIT: LOVING OTHERS THROUGH SACRIFICE

"Teacher, which is the greatest commandment in the Law? And Jesus replied, 'You shall love the Lord your God with all your heart, and with all our soul, and with all your mind. This is the first and greatest commandment, and the second is like it, You shall love your neighbor as yourself. The whole law and the prophets depend on these two commandments.'" (Matthew 22:36–40, NIV)

Loving Others Through Sacrifice

Surrendering to God's agenda in our own personal lives will require a clear view of the "lesser" agendas we so often prescribe for ourselves. The things most people consider important include personal peace, happiness, comfort, prosperity, security, friends, good health, fulfilling experiences, and reaching one's full potential. These agendas, however, often conflict with or ignore God's best plan for us. Our surrender to God's agenda—to His calling—is a statement to the world that we refuse to live for lesser things. Lesser things will not be the things that drive us, but are simply side benefits that come through the sovereign favor and pleasure of God.

The heroes of the faith are the countless people who have surrendered to agendas above and beyond their own. They live with a higher purpose than their own desires and pleasures—they live for others; they are willing to sacrifice their own lives for the lives of others. Many have gone to faraway lands as missionaries. Mothers have sacrificed careers and opportunities for "greater" worldly significance in order to teach their children God's truth. Fathers have altered career plans that conflicted with God's will for their families. Pastors have faithfully served in out of the way places where no one knows their name, and the assignment will never bring them recognition and praise.

> Lesser things are simply side benefits that come through the sovereign favor and pleasure of God.

It is amazing what God can do through one person who is uninterested in his own significance. There is no measure of the impact of one life fully surrendered to God and willing to sacrifice himself for the glory of God. This is the kind of commitment that has marked God's people for generations. Susanna Wesley, whose pastor husband was busy in the ministry and not very involved at home, gave birth to 19 children, of whom only nine lived to adulthood. She raised them, for the most part, single-handedly. It is said that she gathered with her children every day for two hours to read Scripture, pray with them, and teach them the things of God. Her years of faithfulness paid off when God used two of those children, John and Charles Wesley, to bring revival to the British Isles, and fill our hymnals with songs and lyrics that continue to bless us to this day.

If the mind of Christ is to be ours, we must gladly sacrifice ourselves in every area of life to His glory and gain through us. God calls us to surrender to His agenda and to sacrifice our lives for the lives of others. Like Christ, we must be willing to do this in order that God's will might be accomplished through our lives.

The Sacrifice of Christ—Our Example

Philippians 2:6–8 describes the beauty of Christ's example. Christ willingly sacrificed His life in order that God's will might be accomplished through His life. Even though Jesus was God, He did not cling to the privileges of His position. Instead, He willingly emptied Himself. Although we will never understand fully all that His tremendous sacrifice meant, we can see several levels at which He emptied himself to come and redeem us. His example must become ours as we seek to live for God and advance His kingdom.

1. He sacrificed His privileges and rights as the God of the universe. "Emptying Himself" meant that Christ had to give up the voluntary use of many of His attributes. He yielded His omnipresence to be confined in the body of a baby, and He relinquished His omnipotence to endure the cross without overpowering His enemies with the ten thousand angels He could have called down from heaven.

2. He sacrificed the glories of heaven. He willingly relinquished the praise and honor bestowed upon Him by the angelic hosts, all the splendor of what it meant to be Creator, Sustainer and Ruler of the universe— to be born in a lowly stable while the world slept on unaware.

3. Christ sacrificed the pleasures of this life for our sakes. He was willing to sacrifice friendships, being accepted in society and being understood. He sacrificed being loved for who He was, having a place to lay His head, and having money in his pockets.

4. Christ sacrificed most intensely when He gave His body to be hung on a cross like a criminal, carrying the sins of the entire human race upon Him, and dying the death of a despised outcast.

5. Christ sacrificed voluntarily of anything and everything that stood in the way of the glory and gain of His Father through Him.

For us, surrendering to God's agenda and His calling may mean sacrificing our children, our goods, our reputation, our comforts, our convenience, and a whole list of other things we so often hold on to tightly as well as those things we hope and plan for.

The heart cry of the truly redeemed is simply this,

"What can I do to help? How can I use my life and my resources to serve God and others?"

Sacrifice For the Sake of Our Neighbor

Love for others and sacrifice on their behalf is the spirit that Christ brought to this earth. Because He was gladly submissive to His Father and willing to serve His Father's good pleasure, He was thrust into an arena of people with real needs—people hopelessly and helplessly bound for judgment and eternal separation from God apart from intervention. Christ's life was focused on the glory of God and the fulfillment of the Father's agenda. Through our redemption, we too are free to surrender to God's glory, and sacrifice for the sake of others whatever might be standing in the way of our effective service to Him.

The place to start loving God, therefore, is by loving your neighbor! Who is your neighbor? According to Old Testament teaching, *your neighbor is anyone who enters the arena of your existence.* In Jonah's day, it meant strangers, the Gentiles who had converted to Judaism, friends, family and those who lived nearby. It meant the Ninevites! The Pharisees sought to get Christ's opinion as to who their neighbor was, and He included even enemies as He told the story of the good Samaritan. In that parable, *Christ declares that anyone in need—friend or foe—is a neighbor.* And He concludes that neighborly love shows sacrificial mercy upon those who are in need of our help. Ironically, we are always blessed when we invest our lives in the lives of others. This is God's agenda, and we secure His wisdom and blessing when we submit to it.

Sacrifice in Daily Life

Our love of God can be measured by our everyday intercourse with people and the love our interaction displays. Our genuine humility and our willingness to sacrifice for the sake of others is the only sufficient proof that our love of God is real—that humility has indeed taken up its home in us and become our very nature. It is in our relationships to one another, in our treatment of one another, that true lowliness of mind and a heart of humility can be seen. It takes the recognition of our own "nothingness" before God for God to prove to us His power.

Oh, that we might learn from the example of Jonah the danger of our failure to understand this powerful lesson. May we comprehend fully that the ground is level at the foot of the cross. May we see and know that God loves all people and is willing that no one perish. May we understand that He is searching for the one who is willing to submit, surrender and sacrifice for others so that God can highly exalt that one. May we renew our commitment to humility and actively pursue the example of Christ our Lord.

A Parable by Steven James

The disciple went to the temple and laid his life before his Lord. Filled with reverence and awe, he bowed before the altar.

And a voice thundered from the sanctuary, "Leave this place. Leave me. You are no follower of mine."

"But Lord," cried the disciple, "I have been your follower for all these years. I've given to your work, I've abstained from impure thoughts and recited all the prayers that the elders taught me to pray."

"You can't worship me until you know me. You can't know me until you love me. And you can't love me until you've learned to hate yourself."

"Hate? You want me to hate?" the man said. "No, I will not. There's no room for hatred in my religion. You aren't my god after all."

And then he rose and brushed himself off and went away to find a new Lord to worship.

One that made a little more sense.

The most deadly and subtle of all addictions: the infatuation with doing things "my way."

A Prayer for Humility

Father in Heaven,

As I come to the end of the study of Jonah, I am more aware of my pride than I was before I began. Your truth, like a mirror, does that; but Father, it is hard to have such a bright light shining on my inadequacies, fears, failures and sins. Help me, nevertheless, to run into that light, to rise to the challenge of what has been uncovered in my heart through the life of Jonah.

May I cease from the former selfish workings of my heart and mind, and may humility take over. Give me the strength to stop trying to be the god of my life and instead, submit to You as my all in all. Stop me when I attempt to charge forward seeking my own glory or satisfaction. Slow me down when I try to be a savior to others or even to myself. Use my failures to point to Your goodness and sufficiency.

I confess I have specific hopes for my own exaltation. I know what I want it to look like. Help me keep my eyes off of my own hopes and focus instead on You, my only wisdom, my only help, my only hope.

Thank You, Father, for choosing me to be humble and for giving me Your Son as an example of how to acquire it and know it in reality. He is my only hope in this life and throughout eternity for all that you desire me to be. May You one day say to me the words I so long to hear, "Well done, good and faithful servant."

In Jesus' name I pray, Amen.

PAUSE TO PONDER

Principles for Godly Living
Loving Others Through Sacrifice

1. Pride is the root of all sin whereas humility is the root of all virtue.
2. Perhaps the greatest gift God can ever give a man is to finally see himself for what he really is—to see himself as God sees him.
3. The most deadly and subtle of all addictions is infatuation with doing things "my way."
4. Like Christ, we must be willing to sacrifice at all costs in order to prove our love for Him and for our neighbor.

Questions for Life Transformation

1. What question would God ask of you in an encounter such as the one Jonah experienced? What would he pinpoint as your "fatal flaw?"
2. In what ways do your ambitions in life have selfish motives? How does the root of pride affect your genuine love of God and love of others?
3. On a scale of 1 to 10, where is your compassion for those unlike yourself and with whom you struggle? Because you are accountable for the truth you have learned, what will you do to change?
4. Who is that neighbor who needs what you have? Name him or her. What do you plan to do about it?
5. Share the *most* powerful lesson you will take away from the study of the character of Jonah, the character of God.

Story Four: A Recap

God's Greatest Miracle: A Transformed Heart

Perhaps the greatest miracle of this story is that the attitude of Jonah changed. How do we know? The account does not clearly tell us, but most biblical scholars agree that Jonah himself wrote this very personal account. Why would he make himself so vulnerable and transparent to the world and all who would read his account for centuries to come? Why would he present himself in such a negative light and expose his pride and prejudice with no attempt to minimize his faults? Most agree that his account is included in the canon of Scripture in order to show that God's message of love, grace and mercy finally pierced his soul and transformed his stubborn heart! We are led to believe that Jonah's pride and rebellion were finally and forever subdued! *Attempts at ministry are futile without love.*

The story ends with one final question—a question that is left unanswered. It ends in this manner in order that each of us might ask ourselves the same question about eternal issues with which we too so often struggle.

"Is God not right?"

"Is God not great for showing mercy?" (Upon those with whom *we* struggle.)

We are wise to use these questions to examine our own prideful hearts. Like the Ninevites, most followers of Christ are in desperate need of an awakening, and suffer from a deep need to re-prioritize and set into motion a similar progression toward God's light, truth and righteousness.

The lessons from the life of Jonah are numerous. He is a type of practically everything: a type of Christ who was buried, but rose again; a type of Israel who ran from her God-given task; a type of all believers, especially the stubborn ones of us, for we all run away from God at times and are in great need of His discipline. There are lessons that concern powerful nations like Nineveh and the true meaning of awakenings, repentance and genuine revival. There are lessons relating to the doctrine of God's sovereignty over nature and all things, His grace, and His perfect judgment, patience and forgiveness of men. But by far, the greatest of all the lessons to be learned from this tiny book of only 48 verses is the greatness and grandeur of God's mercy in regard to man's stubborn ways. How utterly amazing it is . . .

"There is a wideness in God's mercy,
like the wideness of the sea.
There is a kindness in God's justice,
which is more than liberty.
There is no place where earth's sorrows
are more felt than up in heaven.
There is no place where earth's failings
have such kindly judgment given.

For the love of God is broader
than the measures of the mind
And the heart of the Eternal
is most wonderfully kind.
If our love were but more faithful,
we would gladly trust God's word,
And our lives reflect thanksgiving
for the goodness of our Lord."

Frederick William Faber

But . . . *even* the words of that great hymn are not wide enough. The real measure of the wideness of God's mercy is found in the outstretched arms of the One He sent centuries after the time the historical Jonah lived. The real measure of His mercy is seen in the outstretched arms of Jesus as He hung on the cross to die, offering His own precious blood on behalf of all the sins of all the Jonahs who would follow the one whose life is presented in this story, the Jonah who is a stunning representative of all of us! Christ's death for us is the truest picture we have of the wideness of God's mercy. The cross of Christ is the measure of the length, the depth, the width, and the endless expanse to which the love and mercy of God will go in rescuing and restoring rebellious, stubborn men and women back into favor with our holy and righteous God.

Therefore, after running away from God to Tarshish, next running to God in prayer, then for a time, running with God in Nineveh—finally, Jonah ran *into* a God of incredible love, patience, gentleness, forgiveness and mercy. A God of second chances, third chances and more!

And so, like God's questions to Jonah, there are three probing questions to you, the reader:

1. Just how can you who have known this same mercy and benefited from it, make the choice to be less than merciful to others?
2. How can you do less than love people from every tribe, tongue and nation, and carry this good news of the gospel to them with all the strength and passion you can muster?
3. How many souls might be saved from an eternity of hell and eternal separation from God if only you could learn to see people and love them as God loves them?

"For God so loved the world that He gave His only Son that whosoever believers in Him should not perish but have everlasting life." (John 3:16)

May we be active and engaged participants in the great endeavor of advancing God's Kingdom as we go into all the world making disciples as His representatives, His ambassadors, His missionaries, His messengers sharing the glorious truth of God's grace, mercy and love—His gospel, the very *best* news in all the world!

NOTE

1. Faber, Frederick William. "There's a Wideness in God's Mercy." 1862. Hymnary.org, https://hymnary.org/text/theres_a_wideness_in_gods_mercy. Accessed 27 February 2020.

Conclusion

The Power of Our Choices

From the life of Jonah, we can surely conclude that *disobedience* to God is the pathway to danger, difficulty, discipline and ultimate defeat. Throughout the biblical revelation, the voice of wisdom resounds: *obedience* to God is the key to abundant life and purposeful living. It is only the grace of God's continual presence and power in us that enables us to be effective in advancing His kingdom. Matthew's gospel records the words of Jesus whose teaching emphasizes the consequences of a life of disobedience or obedience:

> "Not everyone who says to Me, 'Lord, Lord,' will enter the kingdom of heaven, but *only he who does the will of My Father* (obedience) who is in heaven. For many will say to Me on that day, 'Lord, Lord, have we not prophesied in Your name, and driven out demons in Your name, and done many miracles in Your name?' And then I will declare to them publicly, 'I never knew you: depart from Me, you who act wickedly and disregard My commands. (disobedience)'"

These words are sobering in their uncompromising intensity. Jesus explains further that one's obedience to God is like building your house (your life) on a rock. When the storms of life come, your house will not be shaken or moved. In stark contrast to a house built upon rock, Jesus shares the opposite truth:

"And everyone who hears these words of mine and does not do them, will be like a foolish man who built his house (your life) on the sand, and the rain fell, and the floods came, and the winds blew, and slammed against that house (life) and it fell, and great and complete was its fall." (Matthew 7:26–27)

Two Biblical Examples of "Crossing the Line"

These statements spoken by our Lord present one of the most difficult truths found in God's word. The question begs to be answered: Is there a line over which, if you pass, there is no return? The answer from God's word is "yes" in more than a few biblical characters. Perhaps Saul, Israel's first king, could be considered a primary example. Because of persistent disobedience to the commands of God, Samuel, God's faithful prophet, was ordered to make the truth of this principle clear to the young king. God commanded Samuel to speak forcefully to Saul saying,

"You have crossed over the line with God, and there is no return for you. Your kingdom has now been taken from you and given to another." (1 Samuel 13:14, author's paraphrase)

In the case of Saul, no amount of remorse could restore the favor of God, for Saul's disobedience to God's commands disclosed a troubling pattern reflecting "the set of his heart." He persistently disobeyed God and his outward sorrow failed to change "the set of his heart." We must continually remind ourselves. The Most High God is all-wise and perfectly just in His judgments. He knew the heart of Saul! With Samuel's shocking announcement, the presence and the power of God's spirit and favor were abruptly removed from Israel's king, and for the remainder of his reign, Saul was left to self-destruction. When God makes a judgment about the heart, we must never doubt His assessment. It is always true, and it remains so. Who are we to question the omniscience of an all-wise and holy God who knows perfectly the heart of every man?

A second example is found in the character of Esau, the twin brother of Jacob, whose story is recorded in Genesis 27. The same assessment is given to Esau as to Saul, and in no uncertain terms. Reading the story, we discover "the set of Esau's heart." Perhaps the writer of Hebrews says it best:

". . . Lest there be any fornicator or profane person like Esau, who for one morsel of food, sold his birthright. For you know that afterward, when he wanted to inherit the blessing, *he was rejected, for he found no place for repentance, though he sought it diligently with tears.*" (Hebrews 12:16–17)

The "set of the heart" is the determining factor for effective leadership and evangelization of God's people. We are God's ambassadors. We represent Him and His character, not ourselves. In all things, we are to glorify Him. Therefore, the character trait of godliness, "God-likeness," is at its core, a matter of the heart—the critical and necessary "set of the heart" that enables one to experience the Spirit's empowering for tasks of eternal impact. In the case of Saul and also with Esau, God's judgment of rejection was precise and accurate. As God cautioned Samuel: "Do not look at his appearance or at the height of his stature, because I have rejected him. For the Lord sees not as man sees; for man looks at the outward appearance, but *the LORD looks at the heart.*" (1 Samuel 16:7)

Jonah: A Reluctant Prophet and a Ray of Hope

Fortunately in the case of Jonah, obviously there was still a ray of hope that the "set of his heart" could finally be changed—that through God's severe discipline of this reluctant but much loved servant, the "set of Jonah's heart" might ultimately come into proper alignment with the will and purposes of God. From the fury of a catastrophic storm into the prison of a great fish, the mercy and patience of God in regard to this wayward servant was relentless. Time and again, Jonah was forced to examine the "set of his heart" and without fail, he was found lacking. By the end of the book, it is obvious he has yet to learn the life-altering lessons of unconditional obedience to the declared will of Almighty God. Over and over he "built his house (life) on shifting sand," defying the command and counsel of the Most High God. He failed to grasp the truth that character problems can potentially cause God's servants to be eliminated entirely from the service of God. Jonah's attitude throughout the course of the four short chapters that record his story reveal that God's judgment regarding his character was absolutely correct. What stands out in stark contrast to Jonah's disobedience is the loving heart of a Father who tirelessly pursues and lovingly disciplines, giving multiple opportunities of grace to realign the wayward heart to His will. Oh, the wideness of His mercy!

Our lives are products of all the choices we make along the way. Choices to listen to God's still small voice, or to ignore it! Indeed, our God is a forgiving God—a God of amazing grace. He can and often does restore the "set of the heart" to Himself. He will cleanse and heal any life that desires, from the heart, total obedience to Him and to His will. He is looking for servants with undivided hearts to be His representatives to a lost and dying world, a world of which Nineveh is a symbol.

"For the eyes of the Lord move to and fro throughout the earth so that He may support those *whose heart is completely His.*" (2 Chronicles 16:9)

Unfortunately the tiny book of Jonah concludes with a question that begs to be answered. Was the "set of Jonah's heart" finally corrected through all he experienced in the span of 48 short verses? The question is left mysteriously unanswered. Doubt lingers in the minds of those who read the story bringing each of us to examine deeply the "set of our own heart" to see what similar character traits of pride may be lurking in us that will, no doubt, potentially eliminate us from God's work of eternal significance and impact. Concluding the book on a negative note obviously leaves the reader wondering: "If Jonah never figured it out, then how can I ever be certain that the 'set of my own heart' is in alignment with the purposes of God for me? Is it even possible for one's heart to be in alignment with God for eternal impact amidst the pressure and pull of contemporary culture with all its challenges?"

A "Heart Set" Pleasing to God

A brief look at the life of one who beautifully exemplified the proper "set of the heart" will certainly inspire us to similar action and impact. A look at the life of William Carey, the Father of Modern Missions, demonstrates powerfully that it is indeed possible to live in our present day with an undivided focus in unconditional obedience to the purposes of God and accomplish great things for God in our own generation.

Carey is a contemporary example of one whose "heart set" pleased God. As the reader leaves this study of Jonah, may God open your eyes to see through William Carey that it is entirely possible to function in this world and fulfill the call of God in a manner that brings the smile of God upon that life. Though dead, Carey still speaks today: Obedience to God is the key to abundant life. Indeed, a commitment to live in obedience to God allows a faithful servant to *"Expect great things from God* and thus, *attempt great things for God!"* These words became the motto of William Carey's life and mission.

Just who was William Carey? He was a pioneer of the modern missionary movement of the West—a movement that reached into all parts of the world; a pioneer of the Protestant Church in India, and the translator and publisher of the Bible into 40 different Indian languages. Carey was an evangelist who used *every* available medium to illuminate *every* dark facet of Indian life with the light of truth. He is the central character in the story of the modernization of the nation of India, for not only did he bring the light of the gospel there, he used every means possible to improve the quality of Indian life in every respect. He is a stunning example of one who loved his God with his whole heart, soul and mind, and he proved that love by loving his neighbors (the Indian people) as himself. The "set of his heart" was pleasing to God, and God used him to make incredible impact upon the world of his day.

In keeping with the character trait concepts studied through the four stories of Jonah, there are four aspects of Carey's *love of God and love of others* that express the "set of his heart."

Carey's Unconditional Love of God

1. Through Surrender

Carey's life-long surrender to God began in the earliest years of his life. Born in August of 1761 in a small village in England, Carey was exposed to the things of God though religious parents who were regular church attenders. As a child, William had an instinctive love for learning and a strong passion for adventure. He was passionately curious about the world, loved to read, and wanted to travel even at an early age. He mastered the languages of Latin and Greek, and developed a discipline of self-study which later benefited him in the tedious work of Bible translations.

After marriage and the birth of his first child, it was obvious that God was in pursuit of this spiritually-sensitive man—at the time, a simple cobbler. The tragic death of Carey's first child, Ann, before the age of two, tendered his heart to the missionary call of God which came, interestingly as he and his wife, Dorothy, experienced this most difficult time of testing.

It was close to midnight as Carey sat at his cobbler's bench reading Captain Cook's book called *Voyages*. As he read, Carey imagined himself standing near the Captain staring up at a wooden cross erected on the shores of an island, placed there as a memorial of an expedition. As Carey looked at the cross, he read further of the Captain's thoughts wondering if missionaries would ever come from some Christian land to tell the natives on this island what the wooden cross stood for. No, the captain concluded, there was nothing to be gained by such an adventure, and he was sure that it would never be seriously thought of, let alone undertaken. Carey, however, was not so quick to dismiss the idea, and as he continued to read, these thoughts simply wouldn't let go. The "roots" of the Captain's words went deep into Carey's soul and forever remained in Carey's heart. These words, in fact, became Carey's "Macedonian call":

"Come over here and help us!"

The Captain's words rang without ceasing throughout Carey's life like a chapel bell challenging the entire Christian church to wake up to the great harvest of souls just waiting for God's messengers to come! Would no one surrender and respond to this great call?

With God's help, Carey would! Then he almost laughed at the thought of himself—a poor, simple cobbler—going to a foreign land as a missionary. Who was he, to challenge the pagan world with the claims of Christ? Single-handedly he could do nothing, but he declined to draw back. He knew that with Christ, nothing is impossible. He refused to run the other way or rationalize that someone else would accomplish this task. Somehow with God's help, he would *surrender everything* and go. He would rouse the Church to hear this same call and answer the great challenge resonating in his heart. Carey's surrender was followed by multiple confirmations, but particularly through a pamphlet written by Andrew Fuller whose words cemented the call of God upon Carey's life: "It is the duty of those who are entrusted with the Gospel to endeavor to make it known among all nations." Carey took these words to be his direct calling from God spoken straight into his own heart. Therefore, in the quietness of that moment, he answered his Master's life-changing summons:

"Here am I, Lord, send me."

And he meant it! With all his heart, with all his soul, and with all his mind! Little did he realize through his *wholehearted surrender*, that he would become not only the Father of Modern Missions, but the Father of the Indian Renaissance of the nineteenth and twentieth centuries. Into the darkness of untouchables, mysticism, the occult, superstition, idolatry, witchcraft, and oppressive beliefs and practices, Carey was providentially called and placed by God to begin the process of India's reform. He saw India not as a foreign country to be exploited, but as his heavenly Father's land to be loved and served, a society where truth, not ignorance, needed to rule. Carey's surrender created a movement culminating in the birth of Indian nationalism and of the nation's subsequent independence. Carey believed that God's image was in man, not in idols;

therefore, it was oppressed humanity that must be served. He believed in understanding the controlling nature instead of fearing, appeasing, or worshipping it; he advocated developing one's intellect instead of killing it, as mysticism taught. He emphasized enjoying literature and culture instead of shunning it. His life and his beliefs focused on justice and love for one's neighbors, and marked the turning point of Indian culture from a downward to an upward trend. The early Indian leaders of the Hindu Renaissance, drew their inspiration from William Carey and the missionaries associated with him. Carey's whole-hearted surrender to God enabled all these things to be birthed.[1]

In *simple childlike surrender*, William Carey's life transformed the nation of India. He lived what he believed, demonstrating the "set of his heart" through his unconditional surrender to God. He *expected* great things from God, and *attempted* great things for God. The record of history reflects in no uncertain terms that indeed, he *accomplished* great things for God. Whereas Jonah failed to love God with all his heart, soul and mind, Carey's life is a model of what surrender really looks like for the one who answers the call of God.

1. Carey understood that *surrender was his choice,* and that his choice to submit his will to God's was proof of his love for God. Loving God begins with a choice to surrender.

2. Carey understood that *surrender is not a one time decision, but a continuous action*—particularly when it is uncomfortable and inconvenient.

3. Carey understood that *surrender is the proper thing to do*. The name "LORD" reveals that God holds the rightful place of authority over us. Submitting to His will, therefore, is the proper thing to do.

4. Carey understood that *surrender is sweet*. It is a positive command that focuses not on duty or activity but on one's intimacy and relationship with Almighty God.

5. Carey understood that *surrender is personal.* We are told to surrender with heart, soul and mind. It is a personal privilege and a daunting responsibility. Refusal to surrender is rebellion against God.

6. Carey understood that *surrender is complete*. The word "all" consumes
   the entirety of who we are. The command is non-negotiable: "Love
   the Lord your God with *all* . . ."
   William Carey loved God through his unconditional surrender.

2. Through Suffering

From early life till his final years, William Carey's life was marked by
suffering—a picture of his Lord Jesus Christ who was Himself a "man
of sorrows." The apostle Paul, perhaps the greatest missionary who ever
lived, wrote from a prison cell Philippians 1:29–30:

> "For you have been granted the privilege for Christ's sake, not
> only to believe and confidently trust in Him, but also *to suffer
> for His sake*, experiencing the same kind of conflict which you
> saw me endure, and which you hear to be mine now."

Paul's list of experiences recorded in 2 Corinthians 11:23–28 never
fails to arouse awe that a human being could love God so much as to
endure so much suffering:

> ". . . with more labors, far more imprisonments, beaten times
> without number and often in danger of death. Five times I
> received from the Jews 39 lashes. Three times I was beaten with
> rods, once I was stoned. Three times shipwrecked, a night and
> day adrift on the sea, many times on journeys, in danger from
> rivers, from bandits, from my own countrymen, from Gentiles,
> danger in the city, in the wilderness, on the sea, among those
> posing as believers, in labor and hardship. Often unable to
> sleep, hunger and thirst, in cold and exposure—and along with
> these challenges—there is the daily pressure of my concern for
> all the churches."

Reading the life of William Carey reminds us of similar challenges
endured for the sake of Christ by Paul. From the beginning, life for William Carey was a challenge. Born into a poor family, he knew firsthand

what it was to live in extreme poverty. He knew what it was like to be hungry, to struggle for simple necessities. He was forced to work to support his family from his earliest years which in the providence of God, prepared him for a lifetime of hard work on the mission fields of India. Answering the call of God, Carey suffered alienation, mocking and misunderstanding from his own family. Even his church was reluctant to send him off with their blessings, as they desired to selfishly "keep him" as their own pastor.

His first few years as a missionary in India were marked by deep suffering on multiple fronts. He lost a second child to fever, watched his wife gradually lose her grip on reality and never return to normalcy. Dorothy, his life partner, was unconcerned for mission work, and slowly drifted into her own world particularly after the deaths of her children, never really becoming the helper to Carey that one doing the work of the Lord so desperately needs. Upon arrival in India, Carey and his family were aliens in this foreign land. Everyone was suspicious of them and many were even hostile to them. The climate, the food, the tropical life, the strain of lengthy travel, disease, fevers and dysentery added to the litany of their never-ending suffering.

Everything conspired to make Carey feel discouraged, dejected and alone, harassed and perplexed. It seemed there was always a pressing need for money, and with little more than a spade by way of tools, Carey was forced to work hard to build his own house of bamboo, tend his garden and support his family. Preaching was not easy, and it seemed sometimes that all was stony ground. Many mocked Carey while others were aloof, apathetic and uninterested. After 25 years of Baptist Mission work, there were some 600 baptized converts and a few thousand more who attended Carey's classes and services, but there were long stretches of time where Carey was overwhelmed, discouraged and doubtful as to his overall effectiveness.

Suffering well for the cause of Christ in this life is perhaps the greatest evidence of one's genuine love of God. To persevere through suffering and refuse to give up when things become difficult is a test of our trust in the goodness of God. To choose to cling to God in times of desperation and distress is a powerful testimony to the sufficiency of God's grace, and an affirmation on the part of the one who suffers that what God allows into the life of the believer is always purposeful and intended for one's best. Loving God means placing one's unquestioning trust in His goodness in all things. As Oswald Chambers state: "If anything, including the closest relationships of a disciple's life conflict with the claims of Jesus Christ, then our Lord requires instant obedience to Himself. Suffering well for Christ means loss of relationships, loss of favor, loss of reputation, persecution and a host of other uncomfortable experiences in this life." William Carey is an outstanding example of one willing to count the cost and move forward in obedience to the demands of genuine discipleship.

Carey's Unconditional Love for Others

3. Through Serving

Carey's love of God evidenced itself in his ever-expanding service to others, particularly the Indian people. He was a British cobbler who became a professor of Bengali, Sanskrit and Marathi at the Fort William College in Calcutta where civil servants were trained. A firm believer in education, Carey began dozens of schools for Indian children of all castes and launched the first college in Asia at Serampore near Calcutta. He had a passion to develop the Indian mind and liberate it from the darkness of superstition. For nearly three thousand years, India's religious culture had denied to most Indians free access to knowledge, and the Hindu and British rulers had gone along with this high caste strategy of keeping the masses in the bondage of ignorance. Carey displayed enormous spiritual strength in standing against the priests, who had a vested interest in depriving the masses of the freedom and power that comes from a knowledge of truth.

His love for the Indian people evidenced itself further as Carey established the first newspaper ever printed in any Asian language because he believed that "(a)bove all forms of truth and faith, Christianity seeks free discussion." His English-language journal *Friend of India* was the force that gave birth to the Social Reform Movement in India in the first half of the nineteenth century.

One of his greatest achievements was his stand against both the ruthless murders and the widespread oppression of women, virtually synonymous with Hinduism in the eighteenth and nineteenth centuries. Carey was a lone voice in India standing for women's rights. The male population in India was crushing the female through polygamy, female infanticide, child marriage, widow-burning, euthanasia and forced female illiteracy, all sanctioned by religion. Carey influenced a whole generation of civil servants, his students at Fort William College, to resist these evils. He opened schools for girls, and when widows converted to Christianity, he arranged marriages for them. It was Carey's persistent battle against sati for 25 years which finally led to Lord Bentinck's famous edict in 1829 banning one of the most abominable of all religious practices in the world: widow-burning. During his professorship, lasting 30 years, Carey transformed the ethos of the British administration from indifferent imperial exploitation to civil service.

Carey's unconditional love of his God sent reflections of light into every area of Indian life he touched—from education, to agriculture, to evangelism, to social justice, to ethics and morality, and beyond. He was a lover of God who used every available medium to illuminate every dark facet of Indian life with the light of God's truth. He is the central character in the story of the modernization of India. His life is a picture of loving his God—heart, soul, and mind—through serving others in every way possible and through every door of opportunity God opened to him.

4. Through Sacrifice

The heroes of the Christian faith are the countless men and women who have surrendered to agendas above and beyond their own. They are people who lived sacrificially, both for God and for others, with a higher purpose than their own. They are willing to sacrifice their lives for God and for others. It is amazing what God can do through just one person with this "heart set"—one who is uninterested in his own significance. There is no measure of the impact of one life fully surrendered to God and willing to sacrifice himself for the glory of God. It is this kind of commitment that marks the genuine servant of God—it is this "set of the heart" that impacts the world for good and for God's glory. If the mind of Christ is to be ours, we must gladly sacrifice ourselves in every area of life. Like Christ, we must be willing to do this in order that God's will might be accomplished though our lives.

For William Carey, surrendering to God's agenda meant sacrificing his wife, his children, his goods, his reputation, his comforts, his home, his convenience and a whole list of other things we so often hold tightly as well as those things we hope and plan for. The cry of Carey's heart continuously was:

"What can I do to glorify you, Lord?"

"How can I allow you to use my life and resources so that Your Kingdom can come on earth as it is in heaven?"

Carey understood that neighborly love shows sacrificial mercy upon those in heed of our help. His genuine humility and willingness to sacrifice for the sake of others was sufficient proof that his love of God was the real thing—that humility had indeed taken up its home within him and become his very nature. Carey was a reflection of the beautiful character of the One he called "Master and Lord." And though dead, still he speaks:

Expect great things from God; attempt great things for God!

Contrasting the life of Jonah, the reluctant prophet, with the fully surrendered life of William Carey leaves the reader to ponder just what it will be like when one day we see Jesus face to face and give an account for the impact or lack thereof of our own contribution to the Kingdom of God. Just how many souls are at stake in our choice to obey or disobey the commands and call of God? God help us to hear, believe, process and apply the powerful life-changing lessons from this book.

When I Stand at the Judgment Seat of Christ

When I stand at the judgment seat of Christ
And He shows me His plan for me;
The plan of my life as it might have been
Had He had His way, and I see
How I blocked Him here, and I checked Him there
And I would not yield my will,
Shall I see grief in my Savior's eyes
Grief, though He loves me still?

Oh, He'd have me rich, and I stand there poor,
Stripped of all but His grace,
While my memory runs like a hunted thing
Down the paths I can't retrace.
Then my desolate heart will well-nigh break
With tears that I cannot shed.
I'll cover my face with my empty hands
And bow my uncrowned head.

No! Lord of the years that are left to me
I yield them to Thy hand
Take me, make me, mold me
To the pattern Thou hast planned.

Alexander Maclaren
1826–1910

NOTES

1. Mangalwadi, Vishal, and Ruth Mangalwadi. "Who (Really) Was William Carey?" *Perspectives on the World Christian Movement*. 3rd ed. Pasadena, William Carey Library, 1999.

2. Mclaren, Alexander. "When I Stand at the Judgement Seat of Christ." *Bible.org*, 2 February 2009, https://bible.org/illustration/when-i-stand-judgment-seat. Accessed 27 February 2020.

Bibliography

Barnhouse, Donald G. *The Invisible War*. Grand Rapids, Zondervan, 1995.

Bishop, Mary Ann. *Servants of the Most High God: Stories of Jesus, the Teaching Ministry and Parables*. Maitland, Xulon Press, 2016.

Briscoe, Jill. "A Carrying God." *Telling the Truth Devotional*, May 29, 2019, https://www.ourdailydevotionals.com/2019/05/29/carried-one-year-devotions-for-women-2019/. Accesed 27 February 2020.

Carlisle, Thomas. *You! Jonah!* Grand Rapids, Eerdmans, 1968.

Chambers, Oswald. *My Utmost For His Highest*. Westwood, Barbour and Company, Inc., 1987.

Chrysostom, John quoted. in Tarrants, Thomas A, III. "Pride and Humility." *Knowing & Doing: A Teaching Quarterly for Discipleship of Heart and Mind*, Winter 2011, http://www.cslewisinstitute.org/Pride_and_Humility_SinglePage. Accessed 3 March 2020.

Drewery, Mary. *William Carey: A Biography*. Grand Rapids, Zondervan, 1979.

Edwards, Jonathan. "Undetected Spiritual Pride: One Cause of Failure in Times of Great Revival." *Harmony Missionary Baptist Church*, http://grace-abounding.com/Articles/Sin/Pride_Edwards.htm. Accessed 27 February 2020.

Ellul, Jacque. *The Judgment of Jonah*. Grand Rapids, Eerdmans, 1971.

Elwell, Walter A. and Philip W. Comfort. *Tyndale Bible Dictionary*. Carol Stream, Tyndale House Publishers, 2001.

Faber, Frederick William. "There's a Wideness in God's Mercy." 1862. Hymnary.org, https://hymnary.org/text/theres_a_wideness_in_gods_mercy. Accessed 27 February 2020.

Haidt, Jonathan. "The Age of Outrage: What the Current Political Climate is Doing to Our Country and Our Universities." *City Journal*, Dec. 17, 2017, https://www.city-journal.org/html/age-outrage-15608.html. Accessed 27 February 2020.

Hession, Roy. *The Calvary Road: The Way of Personal Revival*. Winslow, Buckingham, Rickfords Hill Publishing Ltd., 1950.

James, Steven. *A Heart Exposed*. Grand Rapids, Revel, 2009.

Jeremiah, David. "Swallowed by a Great Fish – Jonah 1:17." *David Jeremiah Study Bible*. Franklin, Worthy Publishing, 2016.

Kaiser, Walter, Jr. "Israel's Missionary Call." *Perspectives on the World Christian Movement*. 4th ed. Pasadena, William Carey Library, 2009.

Keller, Timothy. *The Prodigal Prophet: Jonah and the Mystery of God's Mercy*. New York, Viking, 2018.

"Kikayon." *Wikipedia*, 11 January 2020, https://en.wikipedia.org/w/index.php?title=Kikayon&oldid=935177809. Accessed 18 February 2020.

Lewis, C.S. *The Great Divorce*. New York, Harper Collins Publishers, 1973.

Lewis, C.S. *Mere Christianity*. Harper One, 2015.

Luther, Martin. "Martin Luther's Definition of Faith." *Ligonier Ministries*, https://www.ligonier.org/learn/articles/martin-luthers-definition-faith/. Accessed 3 March 2020.

Mangalwadi, Vishal, and Ruth Mangalwadi. "Who (Really) Was William Carey?" *Perspectives on the World Christian Movement*. 3rd ed. Pasadena, William Carey Library, 1999.

McClung, Floyd. "Apostolic Passion." *Perspectives on World Christian Movement*. 4th ed. Pasadena, William Carey Library, 2009.

McClung, Floyd. *Follow*. Colorado Springs, David C. Cook, 2010.

Mclaren, Alexander. "When I Stand at the Judgement Seat of Christ." *Bible.org*, 2 February 2009, https://bible.org/illustration/when-i-stand-judgment-seat. Accessed 27 February 2020.

Moore, Beth. *Living Free: Learning to Pray God's Word*. Nashville, Lifeway Press, 2015.

Murray, Andrew. *Humility: Read and Reflect with the Classics*. Nashville, B&H Publishing Group, 2016.

Packer, J.I. *Knowing God*. Downers Grove, InterVarsity Press, 1973.

Piper, John. *Let the Nations Be Glad! The Supremacy of God in Missions*. Grand Rapids, Baker Book House, 1993.

Ponraj, S.D. *The Mark of a Missionary: Essential Qualifications for a Missionary*. Chennai, India, Mission Educational Books, 2002.

Ponraj, S.D. *Pioneers of the Gospel*. Revised ed. Chennai, India, Mission Educational Books, 2010.

Sacks, Rabbi Jonathan. *Covenant and Conversation: Genesis—The Book of Beginnings*. New Milford, Maggid Books and the Orthodox Union, 2009.

Scheumann, Joseph. "Five Truths About the Wrath of God." *Desiring God*, https://www.desiringgod.org/articles/five-truths-about-the-wrath-of-god. Accessed 6 March 2014.

Shallis, Marshall, "The Lamb and the Dove" adapted from a sermon entitled *The Calvary Road* by Roy Hession.

Spurgeon, Charles. *All of Grace*. Nashville, B& H Publishing, 2017.

Stott, John R. W. "The Living God is a Missionary God." *Perspectives on the World Christian Movement*. 4th ed. Pasadena, William Carey Library, 2009.

Stowell, Joseph M. *Fan the Flame: Living Out Your First Love for Christ*. Chicago, Moody Press, 1986.

Stowell, Joseph M. *Perilous Pursuits: Overcoming Our Obsession with Significance*. Chicago, Moody Press, 1994.

Stowell, Joseph M. *The Upside of Down: Finding Hope When It Hurts*. Grand Rapids, Discovery House Publishers, 2006.

Tarrants, Thomas A, III. "Pride and Humility." *Knowing & Doing: A Teaching Quarterly for Discipleship of Heart and Mind*, Winter 2011, http://www.cslewisinstitute.org/Pride_and_Humility_SinglePage. Accessed 3 March 2020.

Verkuyl, Johannes. "The Biblical Foundation for the Worldwide Mission Mandate: Contemporary Missiology—An Introduction." *Perspectives on the World Christian Movement*, 4th Edition. Pasadena, William Carey Library, 2009.

Watts, Isaac. *When I Survey the Wondrous Cross*. 1707. Public domain.

Wesley, Charles. "Love Divine, All Loves Excelling." 1947. *Hymnary.org*, https://hymnary.org/text/love_divine_all_love_excelling_joy_of_he. Accessed 2 March 2020.

"What is the Biblical Understanding of the Wrath of God?" *Got Questions*, https://www.gotquestions.org/wrath-of-God.html. Accessed 27 February 2020.

"Who Were the Kings of Israel and Judah." *Got Questions*, https://www.gotquestions.org/kings-Israel-Judah.html. Accessed 2 March 2020.

The Word For You Today. Celebration, Inc., 2018.

About the Author

Mary Ann Bishop is a Bible teacher, author, recording artist and conference speaker. In 1990, Mary Ann became the teaching leader of Bible Study Fellowship in Myrtle Beach, SC, teaching the class 15 years.

Because of her heart for expanding the cause of Christ through global missions, in 2000 she and her husband David established White Harvest Trading Company and White Harvest Foundation, located in Pawleys Island, SC. White Harvest ministries has provided business platforms for missionaries located in China, Vietnam, Laos and Turkey.

Mary Ann regularly travels to India with teams of women who train emerging church planters, pastors and leaders through the storytelling method set forth in her three-volume curriculum series, *Servants of the Most High God* (2010), now published in 10 Indian languages. She has authored numerous resources of biblical characters now in use throughout the mission fields of South Asia.

Mary Ann earned a bachelor's degree from Columbia College and a master's degree from Florida State University, both in music education. She has also completed coursework towards a Master in Divinity at Columbia International University. David and Mary Ann live in Pawleys Island, SC, and are the parents of two grown children and five well-loved grandchildren.

Made in the USA
Columbia, SC
14 August 2020

16418124R00128